THE STORY OF HOCKEY

*A lively history of Canada's national game
—and one of North America's major spectator sports. Here are accounts of hockey's
great rivalries, its superstars and its rough-
and-tumble action.*

PRO HOCKEY
LIBRARY

THE STORY OF HOCKEY

by Frank Orr

Illustrated with photographs

RANDOM HOUSE · NEW YORK

This title was originally catalogued by the Library of Congress as follows:

Orr, Frank.
The story of hockey. New York, Random House [1971]

viii, 143 p. illus., ports. 22 cm. (Pro hockey library, 1)

1. Hockey—History.   I. Title.

GV846.5.O77   796.9′62′09   76–158373
ISBN 0–394–92303–0 (library ed.)   MARC

Library of Congress   71 [4]

Published in the United States by Random House, Inc., New York, and simultaneously in Canada by Random House of Canada Limited, Toronto.

Trade Edition: ISBN: 0-394-82303-6
Library Edition: ISBN: 0-394-92303-0

Manufactured in the United States of America

CONTENTS

Introduction   vii

How the Game Began   2

The Stanley Cup   7

The Silver Seven   12

Play for Pay   17

The Iceman Cometh   23

The House That Smythe Built   27

The Stratford Streak   33

The Gray-Haired Goalie   39

The Longest Games   43

Super-Team in Boston   47

A Rocket Strikes   53

Blue and White Power   58

v

Many Superstars, One Superman 63

The Reluctant Canadien 67

The Russians Aren't Coming, They're Here 71

Hockey's Blackest Night 75

The Great Goalies 79

Gold in Squaw Valley 85

The Golden Jet and the Hawks 89

A Punch in Toronto 93

The Milestone Goals 98

The Reformation of Mikita 103

The Amazing Bobby Orr 108

It's An Old Man's Game 112

Double Or Nothing 116

Will We Ever Beat This Guy? 120

The Greatest Coach 124

Bobby and the Big Bad Bruins 128

From Here to Moscow? 133

Stanley Cup Winners 137

Index 139

INTRODUCTION

The sudden-death overtime period in the fourth game of the Stanley Cup final series between the Boston Bruins and St. Louis Blues on May 10, 1970, lasted 40 seconds.

Boston defenseman Bobby Orr, only 22 years old but regarded as the most skilled player in the history of hockey by many experts, skated towards the St. Louis goal, and accepted a pass from a team-mate. Just as he was up-ended by a St. Louis defenseman, Orr shot the puck. It streaked under the arm of the Blues goalie, Glenn Hall, and into the net for the goal that brought the Bruins the Stanley Cup, hockey's most-prized team award, for the first time since 1941.

Appropriately, that important goal was scored by the young superstar who leads professional hockey into the pivotal decade of its existence—the 1970s. The National Hockey League is moving toward the front rank of North American spectator sports, alongside football, baseball and basketball. Orr's tremendous crowd appeal is an important factor in this ascent.

Orr's overtime goal was the finishing touch to the greatest season of any player in N.H.L. history. During 1969–70, Orr won every available individual award, except the Lady Byng Trophy for "gentlemanly conduct." His most remarkable acquisition was the N.H.L. scoring championship. Until Orr arrived, the possibility of a defenseman becoming top scorer was thought to be as remote as a pitcher hitting the most homeruns in major league baseball.

Since hockey began in the 1850s, the game has held a special place in the culture of Canada. By 1900, hockey was played in almost every small town in the country and its development as a spectator sport was rapid, leading to the early introduction of professional leagues. In the 1960s, telecasts of N.H.L. games earned the highest audience ratings of any program in Canada.

The growth of hockey in the United States was slower. The first American team admitted to the N.H.L., the Boston Bruins, entered in 1924. During the next 20 years, big league teams failed in several U.S. cities, until, in 1942, the N.H.L. became the six-team league (Boston Bruins, Detroit Red Wings, Chicago Black Hawks, New York Rangers, Toronto Maple Leafs, Montreal Canadiens) that existed until 1967. In that year the N.H.L. launched the

After scoring the goal that won the Stanley Cup, Bobby Orr whoops it up. The man behind makes it look as if Bobby has three legs.

most ambitious expansion program of any professional sports league. The Philadelphia Flyers, Pittsburgh Penguins, Minnesota North Stars, St. Louis Blues, Los Angeles Kings, and Oakland Seals were added in 1967; the Buffalo Sabres and Vancouver Canucks joined in 1970.

Hockey, however, remains essentially a Canadian effort. Canada produces more than 95 per cent of the players in the National League, although the growth of American college and high school hockey, and the development of boys' leagues in the U.S., indicates increasing numbers of American-trained players in the N.H.L.

Although the game is relatively new to many Americans, its traditions were created during more than a century of development. That goal of Bobby Orr's was preceded by thousands of others, most of which had a story attached. The best of those stories—from a frozen pond at Kingston, Ontario, in the 1850s, to Orr's heroics in 1970—are here.

THE STORY OF HOCKEY

HOW THE GAME BEGAN

More than 600 years ago men in Northern Europe developed new forms of transport which allowed them to travel more easily over ice and snow. One new invention was the snowshoe, which allowed a man to travel across deep snow without sinking in it. Another was the ski, on which a man could slide easily across the snow. But most important for the story of hockey was the invention of the ice skate. At first men used the small bones of animals as a crude form of skate. Later they used wooden blades. Our word "skate" is thought to come from the Dutch word "schaat," but historians can't agree on whether the Dutch, the Finns, the Swedes or the Norwegians were the first to use them.

Scotland was the country where skating first became a popular sport. In 1572 the iron skate blade was invented, and skating became fun as well as useful. In 1642 the Skating Club of Scotland was organized and soon there were clubs in other countries as well. When people from these countries migrated to Canada as early settlers, they brought their skates, skis and snowshoes with them. In the harsh, long

Canadian winters, this equipment supplied both transportation and recreation for the pioneers.

Ice skates were improved again in 1850 when E. W. Bushnell of Philadelphia invented the steel blade. The new skates did not have to be sharpened frequently as did those with iron blades. Bushnell manufactured the skates and sold them for $30 a pair. Although the price was very high, Bushnell's skates were an immediate success. Soon others were manufacturing steel blades, and skating was on its way to becoming a major sport.

Soon skaters began to develop a simple game to be played on ice. In Canada and the northeastern United States, boys played a game called "shinny" on frozen ponds and rivers. They set up two goals at opposite sides of the ice, using stones as markers. Then they divided into teams. Using homemade sticks, one team tried to hit a block of wood or a ball into the other team's goal. This game gradually became what we know as hockey.

A good "shinny stick" was soon a boy's most treasured possession. Boys would search the forest to find a piece of oak or ash which had a freak growth or root that formed a blade at the proper angle to the handle. The basic rules of "shinny" or hockey had their roots in English field hockey, the Irish sport of hurling and the North American Indian game of lacrosse. The new game had many of the features of the older sports, but it also had new features. Most important, it was played on ice.

An early print shows skaters and ice boats on a frozen bay.

ICE

As the new sport grew, so did its new name, "hockey." Some experts say the word is an English form of the French word "hoquet," a shepherd's stick which resembled a hockey stick. Others claim the word had Indian origins. French explorers who sailed up the St. Lawrence River in 1740 reported

that they saw Iroquois Indians playing a game in which they hit a hard ball with sticks and shouted "ho-gee," meaning "it hurts."

It is thought that a refined game of shinny, with several features of modern hockey, first was played at Kingston, Ontario, in 1855 by members of Her

Majesty's Royal Canadian Rifles, an Imperial Army unit, on the harbor near their barracks. Others claim the game originated in Montreal. Perhaps the first true game of ice hockey with some rules and a limited number of players was played by students at McGill University in Montreal in 1875.

The growth of hockey was rapid. By the early 1880s the game was played in most populated areas of Canada. The early style of play emphasized strength and ruggedness rather than finesse. But soon players learned passing and stickhandling, making hockey a game of skill as well as muscle.

Kingston was the site of the first organized hockey league, founded in 1885 with four teams— the Royal Military College, Kingston Athletics, the Kingston Hockey Club and Queen's University. Leagues quickly were formed in Quebec and Ontario towns, in the prairie provinces and on the west coast of Canada.

Hockey quickly became Canada's number one sport. By 1890 practically every town had its own team and boys had begun to play the game at an early age. Already the game had caused healthy rivalries between towns, and soon large crowds came to watch. These early fans had none of today's luxuries. The game was played outdoors in freezing weather and the spectators bundled up in warm clothes and stood on the ice to root for their favorites. From these hardy beginnings, hockey grew into the game we know today.

THE STANLEY CUP

In 1893 Lord Stanley of Preston, Governor-General of Canada, donated the Stanley Cup to be awarded to the "champion hockey team in the Dominion of Canada." Little did he know that this simple silver bowl would one day become one of professional sport's most treasured prizes. Lord Stanley had arrived in Canada from England in 1888 and immediately became interested in the fast-growing sport. He had built his own rink and frequently was a spectator at games. Near the end of his tenure as Governor-General, Lord Stanley donated the cup, which cost $48.66.

It was to be a traveling trophy: the winning team each year would have possession until a new team won it. In addition, the cup was to be won by direct challenge—a team would have to defeat the team that held the cup directly. At first the Stanley Cup was for amateur hockey teams, since professional hockey had not yet been established. Lord Stanley specified that the first holder of the cup should be the Montreal Amateur Athletic Association team, winner of the Amateur Hockey Association title in 1893.

Lord Stanley of Preston.

The first Stanley Cup match was played on March 22, 1894, between the Montreal AAA and the challengers, the Ottawa Capitals. The game was watched by 5,000 spectators who stood around the rink boards on a raised platform one foot high or in balconies above the ice. Strangely enough, Lord Stanley himself never saw a Stanley Cup game. On his retirement as Governor-General, he had returned to England in May 1893, ten months before the first official playoff for the cup was staged.

Each team in the first cup match had seven

players—goal, point, cover-point, rover and three forwards. The point and cover-point positions were comparable to the defensemen in modern hockey. The rover, as his name implied, roamed all over the rink. The goals were marked by upright posts with no crossbar or net to stop the puck. Montreal defeated Ottawa 3–1 to keep possession of the Stanley Cup and launch one of sport's most emotional, dramatic and successful championships.

Until 1910 the trophy was awarded to the amateur hockey champions of Canada. Then the professional National Hockey Association took possession of it, although amateur teams were still allowed to challenge for it. Since 1926 competition for the Cup has been limited to professionals only—teams in the National Hockey League (NHL).

The Stanley Cup itself has had a strange history. It has been lost, used as a flower pot and even stolen. In 1905 the Ottawa Silver Seven won the Cup. On the way home following their victory party, one member of the team claimed that he could drop-kick it into a canal. Encouraged by his mates, he did boot it into the canal and then the players went home to bed. The next morning they realized the Cup was missing. They returned to the canal and sheepishly fished it out.

The next year the champion Montreal Wanderers had their team picture taken with the Cup in a photographer's studio. When they left, they forgot to take it with them. The photographer's mother filled

The original Stanley Cup. The Cup as it appears today is shown on page 136.

the bowl with earth and planted geraniums in it. Several months later, the Cup was missed and retrieved from the studio window-sill.

Another Montreal team which had just won the Cup was on its way to a victory celebration when their car had a flat tire. The Cup was removed from the car's trunk and placed on the curb while the tire was changed. Then the team proceeded to the party. Later they realized they had lost the Cup. They went back to the place where they changed the tire and found the Cup still sitting on the curb.

During a 1962 playoff series between the Montreal Canadiens and the Chicago Black Hawks, the Stanley Cup was on display in the lobby of the Chicago Stadium. A Montreal fan, who was watching his beloved Canadiens lose to Chicago, left his seat in the third period, pried open the case holding the trophy, and started to leave the arena, carrying the Cup on his shoulder. He was stopped by ushers and police and said that he was taking the Stanley Cup back to Montreal "where it belonged."

Twice in the late 1960s the Stanley Cup was stolen from the Hockey Hall of Fame in Toronto's Canadian National Exhibition Park. Police recovered it undamaged both times, although one robber threatened to toss it into Lake Ontario unless other charges against him were dropped. He probably didn't realize that the Cup had already survived one bath.

The original silver bowl which Lord Stanley donated now is stored safely in a bank vault. A replica sits on top of the new large trophy which was built at a cost of more than $14,000. The names of all winning players since 1893 have been engraved on the Cup at a cost of more than $8,000.

Even a far-sighted man such as Lord Stanley could have no idea in 1893 that his trophy would become so dramatic—and so mistreated—a prize.

THE
SILVER SEVEN

Of all the teams in the early years of hockey, none was more famous or colorful than the Ottawa Silver Seven, Stanley Cup champions from 1903 to 1905. Their star—the first great star in the sport—was Frank McGee. McGee was a great forward who could skate as fast as anyone in his day and scored goals with amazing ease. He also had the ability to dish out punishing bodychecks. During his career he established some scoring records that have never been equalled, including 14 goals in one Stanley Cup game.

If McGee had played in the National Hockey League of the 1970s, he would have become a wealthy man. However, in the early 1900s hockey was strictly an amateur game. A rigidly enforced set of rules prohibited the paying of any money to the players.

In regular season play the Silver Seven dominated the Canadian Amateur Hockey League, which was made up of teams in Montreal and eastern Ontario. However, the Silver Seven's most interesting matches came in the challenge series for the

Stanley Cup. In the Cup matches they faced teams from all parts of Canada.

In the 1902–03 season the Silver Seven first defeated Montreal Victorias to capture the league title. Then they were challenged for the Cup by the team from Rat Portage (later called Kenora) in northwestern Ontario. The series was played in Ottawa in mid-March 1903. A sudden thaw had softened the natural ice surface of the rink, leaving it in poor condition. During one game the puck disappeared through a hole in the ice and couldn't be retrieved. Still, Ottawa defeated Rat Portage in two games to win the Cup.

As defending champions, the Silver Seven were challenged three times during 1903–04, first by the Winnipeg Rowing Club, then by the Toronto Marlboroughs and then by the Brandon Wheat Kings. In some of the roughest hockey ever seen, the Ottawa team beat Winnipeg two games to one, then easily defeated the other challengers.

In the spring of 1904 Ottawa received a challenge from Dawson City in the Yukon. It was early 1905 before the arrangements for a match could be made and the Dawson City team reached Ottawa. The Klondikers travelled from Dawson City to Skagway by dog team, then by boat to Vancouver and by train to Ottawa. It was a journey of 4,000 miles and took four weeks. The Dawson City players, including 17-year-old goalie Albert Forrest, shared the $3,000 cost of the trip, hoping to recover their share of the gate receipts in the series against Ottawa.

The Klondikers had confidence. When they saw the fabled Frank McGee in action during a practice session, one of the Dawson City players said, "McGee doesn't look like much of a hockey player."

McGee scored only one goal in the first game, a 9–2 victory for the Silver Seven. But the second game, which Ottawa won 23–2, McGee scored 14 goals, a record for one game that has never been approached. Eight of those goals were scored in eight minutes and 20 seconds; and three were produced in one 90-second interval. Dawson City was crushed and Ottawa's Silver Seven kept the Stanley Cup.

The Thistles of Kenora (formerly Rat Portage) challenged for the Cup again in 1905. The Thistles, led by forward Tom Phillips, used the new "McCullough" tube skates, the predecessor of the modern hockey skates. The Silver Seven had the familiar flat steel blades. The Silver Seven's McGee missed the first game with an injury and the slick-skating Kenora club ran away with the game. Kenora's Phillips scored five goals as the Thistles won 9–3. Supporters of the Silver Seven were shocked by the defeat.

The second game produced arguments that continued for many years. Because the ice was wet and soft, the thin skate blades of the Kenora players sank into the ice and slowed them down. Some people claimed that the ice was flooded just before the

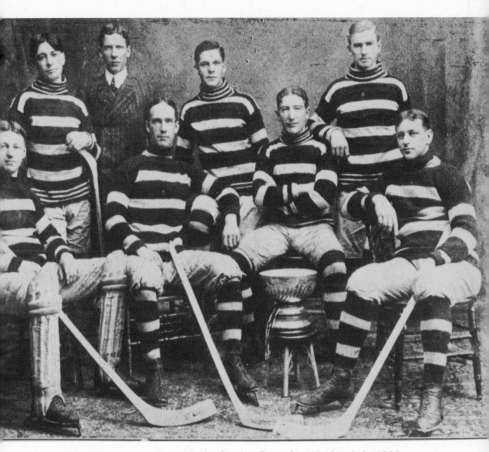

The Silver Seven pose with the Stanley Cup after winning it in 1905. Frank McGee is at far right.

game to soften it; others said that Ottawa supporters had "salted" the surface. Their skating speed greatly reduced by the soft ice, the Thistles resorted to rough hockey, but they lost 4–2 to the Silver Seven.

The third and deciding game of the series turned into a personal scoring battle between Phillips of Kenora and Ottawa's McGee, each of whom scored three goals. When Phillips scored to tie the game 4–4 in the third period, the fans yelled "salt the ice, salt the ice." Then Frank McGee, in true superstar fashion, ended Kenora's hopes of an upset by scoring the winning goal for Ottawa with only 90 seconds left. The Silver Seven had won the Cup for the third consecutive time.

The Silver Seven's domination of hockey ended in 1906 when they were defeated by the Montreal Wanderers. But the team and its achievements form an important part of hockey's history and folklore.

PLAY FOR PAY

As hockey rapidly gained popularity in the early 1900s and rivalry between leagues and teams intensified, it became obvious that the top levels of the game could not remain "amateur" for long. The Federal Hockey League was founded in 1904 with teams in Ontario and Quebec and soon was battling the Canadian Amateur Hockey League for talent. In the war for the top players it was suspected that teams were making illegal payments to keep their stars.

Also in 1904, one league began allowing openly professional players. The Eastern Canadian Hockey Association ruled that professionals and amateurs could play on the same team if the club listed which ones were pros and which ones amateurs. Later these lists were published in the newspapers. In 1908 Tom Phillips, the Kenora Thistles star, said that he was available to any team that would pay him $1,800 for the season. Phillips signed with an Ottawa team.

The first completely professional league was the Ontario Pro Hockey League, founded in 1908 with

teams in Toronto, Berlin (now Kitchener), Brant-
ford and Guelph. Professional hockey was well established in 1910 when the National Hockey Association (NHA), the forerunner of the National
Hockey League, was founded. The Montreal Wanderers, Montreal Canadiens, Renfrew, Cobalt and
Haileybury were the original member teams of the
NHA.

Haileybury and Cobalt were towns in the min-
ing area of Northern Ontario. At first, mine owners
had plenty of money to buy the best available
players. In the small town of Renfrew, another
wealthy man, Ambrose O'Brien, assembled a superb
collection of players. They included Lester and
Frank Patrick, who would make a big mark on the
game, Cylone Taylor, Sprague and Odie Cleghorn,
and goaltender Bert Lindsay. The Patrick brothers
received salaries of $3,000 each, the highest in
hockey history to that point. The costly battle for
players forced small towns such as Haileybury and
Cobalt out of the NHA after one season. To reduce
expenses, the remaining club owners agreed to place
an annual salary limit of $5,000 on each team.

Between 1910 and 1914 several important
changes were brought to the game of hockey. Six-
man teams replaced the seven-player variety as the
rover position was eliminated. Large numerals were
placed on the players' sweaters. This led to printed
programs with names and numbers. In 1914 the
NHA began to keep a record of assists on goals, and

The Vancouver Millionaires brought the Stanley Cup to Canada's western coast for the first time.

the referees dropped the puck on face-offs instead of placing it between the sticks.

Hockey continued to flourish in all sections of the country. The Maritimes Professional League challenged for the Stanley Cup, and the Pacific Coast League was formed by Lester and Frank Patrick. The PCL had teams in Victoria, Vancouver (which had Canada's first artificial ice surface) and New Westminster, British Columbia. Soon a battle for players was being waged between the NHA and the Pacific Coast League. But the two leagues reached an agreement for an annual Stanley Cup series between their champion teams. In 1915 the New Westminster team was transferred to Portland, Oregon, and Seattle, Washington, joined the league a year later.

The new Portland Rosebuds won the Pacific Coast League title in 1916 and became the first team from the United States to challenge for the Stanley Cup. The Rosebuds lost the best-of-five final series to the Montreal Canadiens. The Montreal star was Georges Vezina, their brilliant goalkeeper. The Vezina Trophy, which has been awarded to the top goalie in the National Hockey League since 1927, was donated in his memory.

A battle between owners set the stage for the formation of the National Hockey League. Eddie Livingstone, the owner of the Toronto Shamrocks in the NHA, had purchased Toronto's second NHA team, the Arenas. But the other owners refused to allow him to operate two teams in the same city. Instead of cooperating with Livingstone, the Montreal Canadiens, Montreal Wanderers, Ottawa Senators, Quebec Bulldogs and Toronto Arenas withdrew from the NHA and formed the National Hockey League.

The new league had a disastrous start. First Quebec withdrew, due to lack of fan interest. Then the Westmount Arena in Montreal, home rink of the Wanderers, burned and the team dropped out of the league. The remaining teams—the Canadiens, Ot-

THE ARENA HOCKEY CLUB OF TORONTO

·1918· ·1919·

CHAMPIONS OF THE WORLD

The Toronto Arenas were the first NHL team to win the Stanley Cup. They held it through 1918–19.

tawa and Toronto—operated as a three-club group. The schedule was divided into halves and the winners of each half, the Canadiens and Toronto, met for the league championship. Toronto won that series, then defeated the Vancouver Millionaires to win the Stanley Cup.

The top player in the NHL's first season was Joe Malone, whom the Canadiens had acquired from Quebec when the team folded. Malone scored 44 goals in 22 games, a goal average that has never been equalled. From a difficult beginning, the NHL soon developed into one of North America's most important sports organizations.

The first NHL superstar, Eddie Shore.

THE
ICEMAN COMETH

The National Hockey League changed little in its early seasons. Quebec rejoined the league in 1918, then moved to Hamilton, Ontario, in 1920. The Toronto team changed its name from the Arenas to the St. Patricks.

The first major change came in 1924 when a second Montreal team, the Maroons, and the first United States team, the Boston Bruins, joined the NHL. The Hamilton team became the New York Americans in 1925, and the Pittsburgh Pirates entered the league. In 1926 three new American teams—the New York Rangers, the Chicago Black Hawks and the Detroit Cougars—were admitted and the league began to operate in two divisions, Canadian and American.

In the mid-1920s hockey was trying to gain a foothold in the United States. The game had attracted only slight attention as an amateur game. In order to stay in business, the new American teams needed colorful, exciting players who could attract crowds.

The Boston Bruins had created little interest and

attracted small crowds in their first two seasons. But in 1926 the Bruins acquired the player who was to transform Boston into one of North America's best hockey cities—defenseman Eddie Shore. Art Ross, the Bruins' manager, coach, scout and promotion man, had purchased Shore from a semi-professional team in Edmonton, Alberta. The hard-hitting defenseman quickly attracted attention with his bashing, brawling style of play.

Shore's impersonal approach to everything he did earned him nicknames such as "The Iceman" and "The Machine on Skates." His superb ability and aggressiveness placed him among hockey's best half dozen players of all time. He won the NHL's most valuable player award four times and earned a place on the First All-Star Team six times in his 15-season career. In addition, he revolutionized the role of the defenseman in hockey. In the NHL's early days the defenders had concentrated on protecting their goal and seldom carried the puck. Shore repeatedly took the puck into the attacking zone for plays on the opposition's goal.

He gained fame for more than his great hockey talent. He sometimes played despite injuries that would have sidelined any ordinary man. During his career more than 800 stitches were taken in his face and head. When he was playing Edmonton, Shore suffered a deep cut in his leg in a playoff game against Victoria. It required 14 stitches to close. He traveled to Victoria getting around on crutches.

When his teammates kidded him about faking an injury, he went out and played. Although the stitches came out and blood seeped into his skate, Shore was still the best player on the ice. Another time, playing for the Bruins against Montreal, he played an entire game with three broken ribs and scored three goals.

Shore's brilliant play was often obscured by his hair-trigger temper. The most serious incident occurred during a game against the Toronto Maple Leafs at the Boston Garden in December 1934. The Maple Leafs had two players in the penalty box when Shore led a Bruin power play into the Toronto zone. He was bodychecked at the blueline and knocked down. The Leafs' Irwin "Ace" Bailey was at the Toronto blueline when Shore got up and skated towards him from behind. Shore slammed into Bailey with his shoulder and flipped the Leaf player high in the air. Bailey crashed to the ice head first. It was immediately obvious that he was injured seriously. Then Toronto's big defenseman, Red Horner, rushed at Shore and knocked him unconscious with a right uppercut.

Bailey was close to death for the next month from severe head injuries, and his death was announced erroneously several times. A lengthy investigation of the incident cleared Shore, who claimed he was dazed by the check he had absorbed at the Leaf blueline. But others claimed that Shore had lost his temper when a penalty wasn't called and slammed into the first Leaf he encountered.

Bailey recovered from his injuries, but his hockey career was ended. Later, a benefit game for Bailey was arranged at Toronto between the Maple Leafs and an NHL all-star team. Before the game Shore and Bailey met at center ice, shook hands and embraced to a tremendous standing ovation from the spectators.

Shore never signed a contract in his 15 years at Boston without holding out for more money and he was fined several times following disputes with referees. Although Shore's teammates respected him for his great ability and courage, his cold, arrogant attitude earned him few friends even on his own team. Still, Shore's style—his spectacular rushes and his hard-hitting approach to the game—made him an important factor in the success of hockey in the United States. The spectators didn't love Shore, but in large numbers, they paid their money to watch him play.

THE HOUSE THAT SMYTHE BUILT

Any new enterprise needs men of vision who are willing to take big gambles. The National Hockey League was fortunate to have several such individuals as owners or managers of its teams during the 1920s and 1930s. Conn Smythe of the Toronto Maple Leafs was a king-pin in the growth of the NHL into major league stature.

Strangely, being fired from a job provided Smythe with the inspiration to build his own organization. He worked for Col. John Hammond, who had bought the New York Rangers when the NHL expanded in 1926. Smythe was to be in charge of the new club. He bought and traded players, and was general manager and coach. He did an exceptional job of assembling the first Ranger team. He signed many great players, including goalie Lorne Chabot, defensemen Ching Johnson and Taffy Abel, and forwards Bill and Bun Cook, Frank Boucher and Murray Murdoch. These stars formed the backbone of strong Ranger teams for the next decade. By shrewd dealing, Smythe managed to acquire 31 players for only $32,000, although their value was placed at at least $300,000.

Conn Smythe as he appeared in the 1930s.

Then Col. Hammond fired Smythe from his job as manager-coach before the new team played its first game. Smythe received $7,500 in payment for the severing of his contract, plus a $2,500 bonus for his superb scouting.

When he was fired, Smythe vowed that someday he would organize a team that could beat the one he had built in New York. He returned to his home in Toronto. Toronto's NHL team, the St. Patricks, were in financial trouble. The owners wanted to sell the team for $200,000. Although this was $190,000 more than Smythe possessed, he paid his $10,000 to take a 30-day option to purchase the team. In 30 days he was able to raise $160,000, but he was still short of the St. Patricks' price. Finally, he convinced the St. Pats' owners that they should sell for less money to a Toronto owner rather than sell to out-of-towners who would move the team. Smythe had his hockey team and he immediately renamed it the Maple Leafs.

As hockey interest grew in Toronto, the ancient Arena Gardens, where the Leafs played their home games, became too small to accommodate all the spectators who wanted to see the team. Sometimes several thousand fans had to be turned away.

This convinced Smythe that the city needed a larger arena. The time was 1929. The stock market had crashed and North America was at the start of the depression years. Many businesses were going broke and money for new projects was very scarce. Businessmen thought that Smythe must be crazy to even think about starting the construction of a huge hockey stadium. But Smythe had the vision and ambition to forge ahead with his plans anyway. First he looked for a good location for his arena. Several prospective sites were eliminated when local residents objected to having a hockey rink in their neighborhood.

Finally, he secured land at Church and Carlton Streets in downtown Toronto. Despite the scarcity of money, he managed to raise $1,000,000 to start his project. When he discovered that he was $200,000 short of the money required to finish Maple Leaf Gardens, Smythe convinced the workmen, unions and contractors to accept stock in the building as

part of their wages. Those who accepted the stock prospered when the Gardens became successful. They had made a good investment.

The building of Maple Leaf Gardens was one of the most amazing feats in construction history. On April 1, 1931, the old buildings were cleared from the site. The arena was to be completed by November 12, in time for the first game of the 1931–32 hockey season. Scoffers said the task would be im-

Opening night at Maple Leaf Gardens.

possible, but the opening game was held as scheduled. Smythe always said that the financial interest which many of the workmen held in the building made them work harder to finish it on time.

While the beautiful new arena was being planned and built, Smythe also was building a strong Maple Leaf team to play in it. In 1929 left winger Harvey "Busher" Jackson had joined his former junior linemates, Charlie Conacher and Joe Primeau, to form the famous "Kid Line." Just before the 1930–31 season opened, Smythe completed hockey's first big trade when he secured defensemen Frank "King" Clancy from the Ottawa Senators in exchange for two players and $35,000. Dick Irvin, one of hockey's all-time great coaches, was hired early in the 1931–32 season.

On November 12, 1931, a capacity crowd of 13,542 spectators filled Maple Leaf Gardens to watch the game between the Maple Leafs and the Chicago Black Hawks. Unfortunately, the Black Hawks, who never had won a game in Toronto previously, defeated the Maple Leafs 3–1.

Despite their opening loss, the Maple Leafs won the Stanley Cup that season, sweeping the New York Rangers in three games in the final. Conn Smythe had fulfilled his vow to build a stronger team than the one he had assembled in New York.

The Maple Leafs, who won the Stanley Cup 11 times in the next 40 years, and Maple Leaf Gardens were unqualified successes. The Gardens was filled with spectators for hockey and many other events right from opening night. In fact, since 1946 there has not been an unsold seat for a Maple Leaf game in "The House That Smythe Built."

THE STRATFORD STREAK

Some of the most exciting players in hockey history have been the French-Canadian stars who performed in the red, white and blue uniforms of the Montreal Canadiens. The "Flying Frenchmen" have been the National Hockey League's most exciting and successful team since they joined the league as an original member in 1917. The Canadiens always have featured fast-skating, slick-passing, high-scoring attacks, with the emphasis on offensive hockey. For generations the main ambition of many boys in the Province of Quebec has been to play for the Canadiens.

One of Montreal's greatest players, however, was of German descent and came from western Ontario. His name was Howie Morenz. Morenz joined the Canadiens in 1923 and immediately thrilled the fans with his brilliant play. Other players were faster skaters than Morenz over a short distance, but no player in NHL history could sustain his speed through an entire game as Morenz did. In 550 NHL games Morenz scored 273 goals, won the NHL scoring title twice and the Hart Trophy as most valuable

Howie Morenz.

player three times. Few players in the history of any sport received the adulation that the fans in Montreal heaped on Morenz.

Morenz was born in the little western Ontario town of Mitchell, where he learned to skate and play hockey on the Thames River. "River-hockey" games involved teams with unlimited numbers of players, and often all the players were chasing the puck at once. In such a game only the very best skaters and stickhandlers could keep possession of the puck for long. In this rough-and-tumble game Morenz quickly developed the skills that were to make him such a superb professional player.

When Morenz was in his teens, his family moved to the city of Stratford, where he quickly became an amateur hockey star. He played on as many teams as possible in junior, intermediate and commercial leagues and was a high scorer. Once he scored 11 goals for an intermediate team in a game at Montreal and the next night had six scores for the juniors in a game at Kitchener. Because of his great speed, he was called "The Mitchell Meteor" or "The Stratford Streak."

It wasn't long before the NHL teams were attempting to lure Morenz into professional hockey. Both Toronto and Montreal made him offers. But he had doubts about his ability to play in the NHL because of his size—he was only 5-foot-9 and 165 pounds. Morenz finally relented and signed with the Canadiens. When news of the signing reached Stratford, the local hockey fans placed great pressure on him to stay and they succeeded in convincing him. He wrote to the Montreal team and informed them that he had decided to remain in Stratford. But the Canadiens finally won out. When they threatened to reveal that Morenz had been paid for playing "amateur" hockey in Stratford, he reluctantly reported to their training camp.

The Canadiens' top forward line at the time consisted of Odie Cleghorn at center between wingers Auriel Joliat and Billy Boucher. The Canadiens tried Morenz as center on that line and soon Cleghorn was out of a job. Morenz, Joliat and Boucher blended together instantly and led the Canadiens to the Stanley Cup in 1924. In his first year Morenz had scored 13 goals in 24 games to launch his NHL career in splendid fashion.

Morenz scored 27 goals in his second season. All of Montreal was excited by his spectacular end-to-end rushes, his combative but gentlemanly style of play and his slick passing. The Canadiens' attendance soared to new highs and Morenz was recognized wherever he went. Morenz and the Canadiens also attracted big crowds in other NHL cities at a time when the game was struggling for recognition. When the Canadiens visited American cities, the arenas were packed. Everyone wanted to see the "Flying Frenchmen" and their spectacular star.

In 1934 Morenz was traded to the Chicago Black Hawks. The trade was a huge shock to everyone, especially to Morenz. He had led the Canadiens to Stanley Cup victories in 1929 and 1930 and was the NHL's most valuable player in 1931 and 1932. But he had scored only eight goals during the 1933–34 campaign and Montreal decided to trade him. The shocked Morenz walked the streets of Montreal all night after hearing about the trade, and early the next morning his wife found him sitting on the living-room floor with tears running down his cheeks.

Morenz was extremely unhappy in Chicago because the Black Hawks played a conservative, defensive game. After one season he asked to be traded and Chicago sent him to New York. There Morenz was frequently involved in arguments with his mates and his play was ineffective. The Canadiens purchased Morenz from New York in 1936 and reunited him with his old linemate Joliat and Johnny Gagnon, Boucher's replacement. Although 34 years of age, Morenz showed flashes of his old form and the fans showered him with the familiar cheers.

On January 28, 1937, Morenz' left leg was broken in two places in a game against Chicago when an opposing player fell on it. He was rushed to the hospital where his leg was placed in a cast. His fans and teammates flocked to visit him and Morenz talked of a comeback when his leg healed. But he grew depressed in the hospital, worrying about his leg and his lack of money—although he had been well-paid, he had saved little. Within a month Morenz suffered a nervous breakdown. On March 8 he tried to get out of bed and fell to the floor. He was dead by the time a doctor arrived.

The doctors claimed he died of heart deficiency and acute excitement. His friends claimed Howie Morenz had died of a broken heart because he had never recovered from being traded away from his beloved Montreal. His body was placed at center ice in the Montreal Forum and long lines of fans filed past to pay their last respects. His number "7" was retired permanently by the Canadiens.

THE GRAY-HAIRED GOALIE

Although he spent almost 50 years in hockey as a player, coach and manager, and compiled a distinguished record in all roles, Lester Patrick is best remembered in hockey circles as "the gray-haired goalie."

Patrick had been one of hockey's top players in the game's early days. He played rover until that position was abolished when hockey became a six-player game. Patrick switched to defense but retained his scoring eye. In 208 games of professional hockey he scored 130 goals.

Lester and his brother, Frank Patrick, were members of the famous Renfrew Millionaires team which joined the National Hockey Association in 1910. When the Renfrew club folded, the Patricks headed west and formed the Western Canada League. Lester Patrick was a player-coach with several clubs in that league.

In 1926 Patrick succeeded Conn Smythe as manager-coach of the New York Rangers in that club's first season in the National Hockey League. He held both jobs until 1939, then gave up coaching

and continued as the Ranger general manager until
1946. His teams won three Stanley Cup titles and
Patrick was voted into the Hockey Hall of Fame as a
player in 1945.

Despite these accomplishments, Patrick's name
usually is associated with his one-game goaltending
stint during the 1928 Stanley Cup finals. In this series the Rangers faced the Montreal Maroons. New
York had won the American Division playoffs, while
the Maroons had taken the playoffs in the Canadian
Division.

The Maroons won a hard-fought 2–0 victory in
the opening game of the best-of-five series. The second game, at Montreal, was scoreless through the
first period. Early in the second period the Maroons'
star forward, Nels Stewart, fired a backhand shot
that struck Rangers' goalie Lorne Chabot over the
eye, knocking him to the ice. He was bleeding pro-
fusely and was taken to the hospital. Chabot's importance to the Rangers was shown by his performance during the season. In 44 games he had scored
11 shutouts and permitted only 1.79 goals against
per game.

The Maroons insisted on a strict interpretation
of the rule regarding substitute goalies. The rule
stated: "In the event of a goalie sustaining injury, he
will be allowed ten minutes to recuperate. If unable
to continue, his team must put on a substitute, a substitute being interpreted as a player under contract."
New York wanted to use Ottawa's goalie, Alex Con-

nel, who was at the game as a spectator, but Montreal refused permission. Then the Rangers suggested Hugh McCormick, a minor league goalie, but Montreal refused again.

Following a long delay and several heated arguments between the teams, Patrick decided to play goal himself. He was 44 years old and had been out of fulltime duty as a player for several years. Patrick dressed in the goaltender's equipment, pulled a

Gray-haired Lester Patrick poses in front of the goal.

baseball cap over his silver hair and skated onto the ice for a warmup. The Montreal crowd hooted.

The Rangers checked hard to protect their elderly goalie. But some shots got through and Patrick spent much time on his hands and knees as he fell down to stop them. During his days as a defenseman in the Western League, Patrick had been famous for stopping shots by falling to his knees in front of them, earning the nickname "The Praying Colonel."

In the third period Ranger star Bun Cook gave New York a 1–0 lead. The Rangers increased their checking, trying to protect their lead and their goaltender. However, once after Patrick had fallen to his knees, Stewart of the Maroons lifted the puck over him and into the net to tie the score.

The game went into sudden-death overtime. And after seven minutes, five seconds of the first overtime period, Ranger Frank Boucher, who later succeeded Patrick as the team's coach and manager, scored the winning goal for the Rangers.

The Ranger players mobbed Patrick when the game was over and almost carried their exhausted goalie to the dressing room. Patrick had stopped 18 shots on goal and earned a place in hockey history. Fortunately for Patrick and the Rangers, Chabot's injuries were not serious. He returned in the third game and helped the Rangers win their first Stanley Cup crown.

THE
LONGEST GAMES

Although regular-season games can end in a tie and often do, ties are decided by sudden-death overtimes in Stanley Cup playoff games. In overtime the game ends when the first goal is scored, producing a dramatic situation that is matched by few in any sport. Spectators are afraid to take their eyes away from the action for even a moment for fear they will miss the critical play.

Throughout the history of the National Hockey League, overtime games have produced some famous incidents. Many of the NHL's great stars have scored important overtime goals, but several little-known players have also gained fame by scoring a winning goal in extra time.

Ken Doraty of the Toronto Maple Leafs and Moderre "Mud" Bruneteau of the Detroit Red Wings certainly were not NHL superstars. Doraty spent four seasons in the NHL and scored only 19 goals. Bruneteau was a solid, unspectacular defensive forward during his 11 seasons. He scored 139 goals in 399 big league games. But because of the overtime goals they scored during the 1930s, Doraty and Bruneteau gained places in hockey history. Their scores decided the two longest games ever played.

During the 1933 Stanley Cup playoffs, the Maple Leafs and the Boston Bruins were involved in a very close semi-final series. Three of the first four games in the series had required overtime. The fifth game, at Toronto, saw a continuation of the close-checking play and the game was a scoreless tie after 60 minutes of regulation time.

The teams battled through five 20-minute over-time periods with neither team able to score. In the fifth overtime period the pace of play was extremely slow with only occasional bursts of action. The players were exhausted, having played two-and-a-half hours of hockey. However, few spectators in the capacity crowd at Maple Leaf Gardens left the building.

After the fifth overtime the team managers—Art Ross of Boston and Toronto's Conn Smythe—asked NHL president Frank Calder to stop the game and finish it the following night. Calder refused. A coin toss was suggested to decide the winner. Although the players were willing to use this method, the crowd booed loudly when it was announced. When Calder suggested that both teams remove their goalies for the sixth overtime period, the managers objected. So play continued under regular rules.

The sixth overtime period opened with some lively action that surprised the spectators. In the

fifth minute of play Toronto's Andy Blair inter-
cepted a pass from Boston's great defenseman Eddie
Shore and slipped the puck to Doraty, who, at 5-
foot-7 and 133 pounds, was one of the smallest
players in NHL history. Doraty raced towards the
Boston net and slid the puck past goalie Tiny
Thompson to give the Maple Leafs a 1–0 victory.
The goal came after 164 minutes, 46 seconds of
hockey, and ended the game at 2:25 a.m.

The exhausted Leafs had to open the final series
against the New York Rangers only 18 hours later.
New York won the game easily and continued on to
a Stanley Cup triumph.

Doraty's goal ended the longest NHL game
played up to that point. However, the record didn't
remain in the books for long. The opening game of
the semi-final Stanley Cup series in 1936 saw two
goalies—Lorne Chabot of the Montreal Maroons
and Normie Smith of the Detroit Red Wings—play
brilliantly as the teams failed to score in regulation
time.

The overtime session produced some wide-open,
exciting hockey and the fans expected one of the
teams to score quickly. But Chabot and Smith
couldn't be beaten through five 20-minute overtime
periods.

Playing for the Red Wings in his first Stanley
Cup game, Mud Bruneteau had seen only limited
action in the first 160 minutes of play. He had spent
most of the 1935–36 season with the Red Wings'

farm team, the Detroit Olympics, in the semi-professional International League. The Wings promoted him halfway through the season and he had scored only two goals in 23 NHL games.

Bruneteau came into the game more often as the overtimes progressed, since the Red Wing regulars were exhausted. Late in the sixth session, after 176 minutes, 30 seconds of play, Bruneteau's 25-foot shot eluded Chabot to give the Red Wings the victory.

With their single dramatic goals Doraty and Bruneteau acquired more fame than many players who scored 300 or more goals during their NHL careers.

SUPER-TEAM IN BOSTON

A favorite pastime of hockey fans is debating about which was the greatest team in the National Hockey League. Every fan has his choice as the all-time greatest club, even though no final decision can be made because there is no way to compare teams from different eras of the game.

A consensus of expert hockey opinion narrows the selection down to a few clubs—the Toronto Maple Leafs of the late 1940s, the Detroit Red Wings of the early 1950s, and the Montreal Canadiens of the late 1950s and the mid-1960s. However, many experts vote for the Boston team of the 1937-to-1941 period. Starting with the 1937–38 season, the Bruins finished in first place for four years in a row and won the Stanley Cup twice.

The Bruins of that era had all the necessary ingredients of a championship club—excellent goalkeeping, a strong, mobile defense, and a balanced attack consisting of three forward lines of players who could both score and check. The team was masterminded by the brilliant manager-coach Art Ross, one of hockey's greatest tacticians and innovators.

Ross had carefully built the Bruin team through good scouting of young Canadian amateur players, a strong farm system and some shrewd deals. During the 1930s the Bruins, led by the incomparable Eddie Shore, had been consistent contenders for first place and the Stanley Cup, but late in the decade they began to take shape as a super-team.

In 1936 the Bruins acquired the famous "Kraut Line" of center Milt Schmidt and wingers Woody Dumart and Bobby Bauer from the Kitchener, Ontario, junior team. Because all three players were of German descent, the "Kraut" nickname was given to them immediately. Schmidt quickly became the Bruin leader with his hard-driving play and tough bodychecking.

During the next three seasons the parts fell into

The "Kraut Line," Milt Schmidt, Woody Dumart and Bobby Bauer, with Boston Manager Art Ross.

place to give Boston the NHL's best team. Slick center Bill Cowley joined wingers Roy Conacher and Mel Hill on a forward line that rivalled the "Krauts" in offensive strength. Ray Getliffe, Red Pettinger and Red Hamill contributed forward depth.

Although Shore was nearing the end of his magnificent career, he won the NHL's most valuable player award in 1937–38 and joined Flash Hollett, Dit Clapper, Johnny Crawford and Jack Portland on perhaps the strongest defense in the league's history. The Bruins finished first in the league but the Chicago Black Hawks won the Stanley Cup playoffs.

In the 1938–39 season the Bruins added the final block in the construction of their team. Goalie Frank Brimsek, a native of Eveleth, Minnesota, was brought up from the Bruins' Providence farm team to share the goaltending job with veteran Tiny Thompson. Early that season Ross took a big gamble when he traded the reliable Thompson to Detroit and gave the first-string job to Brimsek. Some Boston fans were critical of the trade but Brimsek's superb play quickly silenced them. He won the Vezina Trophy as the NHL's leading goalie with a 1.59 goals against average and also won the Calder Trophy as top rookie. He was soon known to the fans as "Mr. Zero."

The Bruins finished in first place, 16 points in front of the New York Rangers. The team scored 156 goals in 48 games and yielded only 76. Although

A hand-made poster of the 1938–39 Bruins.

the team's scoring attack was well balanced, Roy Conacher led the NHL with 26 goals. Physical strength was an important part of the Bruin success. Most players on the roster were big, and although they weren't especially belligerent, their stamina allowed them to wear down their foes with hard checking.

In the semi-final of the Stanley Cup playoffs, the Rangers gave Boston a good battle, but the Bruins won the series in seven games. Three of the games required overtime, and in each one Boston's Mel Hill scored the winning goal, earning the nickname "Sudden-Death." Sparkling play by the young line of Schmidt, Dumart and Bauer led the Bruins to victory in the final against the Toronto Maple Leafs. Boston won four of the five games to capture the Stanley Cup.

Manager Ross didn't stand pat with his championship club. The following season, Shore was sold to the New York Americans. Defensemen Des Smith and Terry Reardon and forwards Art Jackson and Herbie Cain were added to the team.

Boston's domination of the NHL continued in the 1939–40 season. Schmidt, Dumart and Bauer finished one-two-three in the scoring race, Cain scored 21 goals and the Bruins finished in first place. However, even the great depth of talent on the Boston roster couldn't overcome a lengthy injury list in the playoffs. Clapper, Hill, Jackson and Smith were on the sidelines as the New York Rangers eliminated Boston in a six-game semi-final series.

In 1940–41 the Bruins again finished in first place and established two records that never have been equalled—the longest-winning streak, 14 games; and the longest undefeated streak, 23 games (15 wins, 8 ties). Center Cowley was the NHL's leading scorer with 17 goals and 45 assists. The Bruins and the Toronto Maple Leafs fought through a close semi-final series for the Stanley Cup. Then in the seventh game Boston took a 2–1 decision as Mel Hill scored the winning goal. Boston then swept Detroit aside in four games to win their second Stanley Cup in three seasons.

The Bruins' domination of the NHL might have continued for several years. But World War II had begun and many of Boston's young stars left hockey to enter the armed forces. The super-team had been broken up.

A ROCKET STRIKES

The years of World War II (1939 to 1945) were trying ones for the National Hockey League. Many players had traded their hockey uniforms for armed forces dress. Most of those who remained were very old or very young and teams had to struggle to continue their operation. One of the first NHL personalities to be conscripted for war duty was Conn Smythe, the owner-manager of the Toronto Maple Leafs. He became Major Smythe, Commanding Officer, 30th Field Battery, 7th Toronto Regiment, Royal Canadian Artillery. Smythe was one of Canada's most decorated soldiers for his bravery in service and many NHL players served in his regiment.

In 1942 more than 90 NHL players were in the service and there was talk of disbanding the league. But the Canadian and United States governments agreed that hockey was good for national morale, so the NHL continued despite the scarcity of good players. The teams struggled through with service rejects, teenagers and some older players.

The New York Rangers had more problems than any other team. Their roster of regulars was ravaged by the Armed Services call. In the three seasons from 1942 to 1945 the Rangers won only 28 games. During 1943–44 they had only six wins and five ties in 50 games.

The 1943–44 season was an important one in NHL history, however, for that was the year Maurice "Rocket" Richard arrived as a big league hockey star. Richard had joined the Canadiens the previous season, but had suffered a broken ankle early in the schedule. In '43–44 he scored 32 goals and 22 assists during the schedule. Then he added 12 goals in nine playoff games as the Canadiens won the Stanley Cup. In one semi-final game against Toronto, Richard scored five goals in a 5–1 win by the Canadiens.

Thus, one of the NHL's most remarkable and

Maurice "Rocket" Richard skates on the boards to get around New York Ranger Allan Stanley.

controversial careers was launched. Despite a long list of crippling injuries, Richard scored 544 goals in his career (which lasted through 1959–60), plus a record 82 playoff goals.

Scoring was only a part of the Richard story. His quick temper and the incidents that it caused soon became legendary. Off the ice, Richard was a quiet, very shy man. But when he donned the uniform of his beloved Canadiens, he became a bombastic, explosive player whose frequent outbursts against opponents and officials earned him many fines and suspensions.

Richard was perhaps the most intense competitor and perfect team player in the history of the NHL. He never was happy unless the Canadiens won. When he scored the 600th goal of his career, including playoffs, against New York in 1958, Richard said, "The only goals I remember are the ones that win games for the Canadiens." Richard teamed with center Elmer Lach and left winger Toe Blake to form the famous "Punch Line." During the 1944–45 season the trio totalled 105 goals. Richard set an enduring record by scoring 50 goals in 50 games.

Richard produced some of the NHL's most dramatic goals, including many overtime winners. In the 1950–51 playoffs he counted three overtime goals. During the 1957–58 Stanley Cup final the Canadiens and the Boston Bruins were tied at the conclusion of regulation time. In a television inter-

Richard attempts to score against Chicago goalie Al Rollins.

view before the overtime period, Montreal's managing director Frank Selke was asked to predict the outcome. He said that Rocket Richard would score the winning goal. Richard did score on a spectacular effort.

Richard suffered several crippling injuries, especially near the end of his career. However, he would return from a long period on the sidelines and immediately produce flamboyant goals. On November 14, 1957, he sustained a severed Achilles tendon and was out of the lineup until February 21, 1958. In his first game back Richard scored two goals. In January, 1959, he broke his ankle and his career appeared to be finished. But he returned for the playoffs and helped the Canadiens win the Stanley Cup.

The 1959–60 season was Richard's finale in the NHL. He was 38 years old, but his competitive fire burned as brightly as ever. Although a broken cheekbone limited his action to 51 games, he scored 19 goals and led the Canadiens' charge to their fifth consecutive Stanley Cup triumph. When Richard announced his retirement in September 1960, he held 17 NHL scoring records. He had anchored eight Stanley Cup champion teams and was named to the All-Star Team 14 times.

"Hockey was the only thing that ever really mattered to the Rocket," a teammate once said. "He felt the Canadiens represented the French-speaking citizens of Canada, and if he didn't play well, he disgraced his people."

BLUE AND WHITE POWER

When World War II ended and the National Hockey League players returned from the armed forces, the league entered a period of superb competition. During the wartime player shortage many youngsters had been brought into the NHL duty while in their teens. By 1946 the league had both the old pros back from the war and the youngsters, who had matured into solid NHL performers.

During the war years the Toronto Maple Leafs had won the Stanley Cup twice (1941–42, 1944–45). When they combined their returned veterans and their young wartime players, they had a superb roster. With Conn Smythe as manager and Clarence "Hap" Day as coach, the Leafs swept to three consecutive Stanley Cup titles from 1946–47 to 1948–49, and added another in 1950–51. The basic roster remained the same through that five-year stretch of blue-and-white excellence, although Smythe's shrewd dealing bolstered any potential weak spots.

A graduate pharmacist, Hap Day had been a great Maple Leaf defenseman during the 1930s. As a coach, he was a hard-driving taskmaster who demanded perfection in hockey's fundamentals. His teams excelled in two departments—physical conditioning produced by strenuous workouts, and defensive play.

"In hockey, it's not the things you do right that win for you, it's the things you do wrong that beat you," Day once said. "The team that makes the fewest mistakes usually wins."

The trademark of the Day teams was their checking ability. Some of the most powerful attacks in hockey history were obliterated by the blanket backchecking of the Maple Leafs. The team was known as "the clutch and grab champions of all time" because of this close-checking approach. Although Day's detractors claimed his teams played dull hockey to watch, no one argued about its effectiveness. Players who would have been high scorers with an offensive-minded team had to fit into the Day system. If they didn't, they were traded. The post-war Leaf teams had no "fringe" players. Every member of the club was a strong individual performer.

The key Leaf player was goaltender Walter "Turk" Broda, whose portly physique led to his nickname: "The Fabulous Fatman." Broda didn't use the standup style of most great goalies. Frequently he flopped to the ice to block shots. He was particularly effective during playoff games. "When the playoff money was on the line, Turk was the best," commented manager Smythe. "Put a dollar in front of him and Broda could catch lint in a hurricane."

The Leaf defensemen—Garth Boesch, Gus Mortson, Jim Thomson and Bill Barilko—were not noted for their puck-carrying, but they all were solid bodycheckers, poised positional players and skilled passers.

Few teams in history could match the large number of excellent two-way forwards that the Leafs could ice. Centers Syl Apps and Ted Kennedy, wingers Wild Bill Ezinicki, Harry Watson, Howie Meeker, Vic Lynn, Nick and Don Metz and Joe Klukay provided good scoring depth and strong defensive ability.

In the 1946–47 playoffs the Leafs, who had finished second to Montreal during the regular schedule, started their string of Stanley Cup victories by eliminating Detroit and then defeating Montreal for the Cup. Broda yielded only 27 goals in 11 games.

Despite the Cup win, Smythe was not satisfied with his team. He figured the Leafs needed another strong center to team with Kennedy and Apps. Just before the 1948–49 season he completed the biggest trade in NHL history when the Leafs acquired Max Bentley, one of the league's best centers, and unknown Cy Thomas from the Chicago Black Hawks in exchange for five players.

Bentley completed an outstanding roster and was the Leafs' leading scorer as the team finished in first place in 1948–49. The team had everything—fine goaltending from Broda, a solid defense, three balanced forward lines, strong penalty-killing and a good power play, plus the disciplined approach to the game produced by Day's hard-driving technique. Toronto faced only token resistance in the playoffs, sweeping Boston aside in five games before eliminating Detroit with four consecutive victories to win the Stanley Cup.

The retirement of Apps before the 1948–49 season deprived the Leafs of a superior center, but Smythe secured Cal Gardner in a trade to replace him. Still, the Leafs slipped to fourth place during the season, 18 points behind first-place Detroit. Then Broda displayed his super-powers once again in the playoffs. The aging, chubby goalie allowed only 15 scores in nine games as the Leafs eliminated Boston and Detroit to win their third consecutive Stanley Cup.

Detroit ended the Toronto reign in the 1949–50 season, sidelining the Leafs in a hectic seven-game Stanley Cup series. But Toronto bounced back to win its fourth Stanley Cup in five years in 1950–51. The Leafs finished second during the regular season and eliminated the Boston Bruins in the semi-final. This sent Toronto against Montreal in a frantic final series in which all five games were decided in overtime. The Leafs won four of the games.

The fifth and deciding game of the series was one of the most dramatic in hockey history. The Cana-

Bill Barilko scores the goal that won the Stanley Cup for Toronto in the 1950–51 playoffs.

diens were in control of the game, but Broda's superb goaltending held them to a 2–1 lead late in the game. In the final minute of play the Leafs took Broda out for a sixth attacker and winger Tod Sloan managed to tie the score. When the game went into sudden death, big veteran defenseman Bill Barilko won the Stanley Cup for Toronto with a hard slap-shot from the blueline that caught the upper corner of the Montreal net. The following August Barilko died in the crash of a private plane in Northern Ontario.

With that thrilling Stanley Cup victory the reign of the Maple Leafs came to an end. They had been one of hockey's all-time great teams, but it was time for them to give way to another super-team—the Detroit Red Wings led by Gordie Howe.

MANY SUPERSTARS, ONE SUPERMAN

In any list of the great athletes in the history of sports, Gordie Howe, the marvellous right winger of the Detroit Red Wings, must rank at or near the top. He entered the NHL in 1946 and 25 years later he continued to turn in great performances. No other athlete in a strenuous, contact sport had been able to play in the front ranks of his game for so long.

The NHL record book is Howe's personal property. He has played more games, scored more goals, acquired more assists and more scoring points than any other player. He has won the NHL scoring title six times, won the Hart Trophy as most valuable player six times and has been named to the All-Star Team 21 times, 12 times to the First Team.

Any notion that his great talent was dwindling was scuttled by his 1969–70 performance when he had 31 goals and 40 assists and earned the right wing selection to the First All-Star Team. Howe's competitive spirit remained high and his reputation as the toughest player in hockey remained almost unchallenged.

Born in the tiny Saskatchewan village of Floral, Howe played his first hockey in Saskatoon, where his family moved when he was nine. Tall and clumsy, he attended a New York Ranger tryout camp at 15, but was discouraged and returned home. A Detroit scout recommended Howe to the Red Wing manager, Jack Adams, and Howe attended a Detroit training camp the next year. Adams spotted the great potential in the young Howe and dispatched him to the Galt, Ontario, jun-

Gordie Howe (*center*).

ior team. A year later, at 17, Howe became a professional with Omaha in the old United States League and scored 22 goals.

In 1946 Howe cracked the Red Wing line-up, scored seven goals in his rookie season and launched the greatest career in hockey history. In his third season he was Second All-Star Team right winger and leading scorer in the playoffs. In the 1948–49 season the Red Wings, led by the young Howe, commenced one of the NHL's most amazing streaks. During the next nine seasons Detroit finished in first place eight times and won four Stanley Cups.

Howe teamed with lanky center Sid Abel and aggressive little left winger Ted Lindsay to form the "Production Line," a potent combination for many seasons. Goalie Terry Sawchuk, defensemen Red Kelly, Bob Goldham and Marcel Pronovost, and forwards Glen Skov, Tony Leswick, Marty Pavelich and Alex Delvecchio gave the Wings a superb line-up of stars.

The key performer was Howe. He cracked the 40-goal barrier in the 1950–51 season when he won his first of four consecutive scoring titles. He also established himself as hockey's best in physical combat, quickly revenging any fouls committed against him. Some opponents called him "the dirtiest player in hockey."

"I'm aggressive, not dirty," Howe said. "You certainly don't try intentionally to injure anyone."

Opposing players quickly learned to save their

illegal tactics for someone else and Howe was able to play in relative freedom from harassment. In the later years of his career only rookies dared to test him and they soon learned that it was not worthwhile.

Big (6-foot, 205 pounds), slope-shouldered and incredibly strong, Howe was a master of every hockey skill. An easy skater whose blades barely cleared the ice between strides, Howe learned to pace himself so that he could play 40 minutes per game. He was completely ambidextrous and could deliver a forehand shot from either side. His wrist shot, delivered with a mere flick of his big wrists, was once measured at 114.2 miles per hour, compared to 118.3 miles per hour for the hardest slapshot.

On November 11, 1963, Howe became the NHL's all-time scoring leader when he scored his 545th goal, passing Maurice Richard of Montreal. During the 1950s when both were in their prime, hockey fans argued loud and long about who was better, Howe or Richard. Richard may have been the more dynamic, but ten years after he retired, Howe was still going strong. Howe's amazing durability had given him nearly all of hockey's career records, some of which may never be equalled.

THE RELUCTANT CANADIEN

When he was a boy in Victoriaville, Quebec, Jean Beliveau shared the ambition of most French-Canadian lads: he wanted to play hockey for the Montreal Canadiens. Unlike most others, Beliveau realized his ambition. From the time he joined the Canadiens in the 1953–54 season, Beliveau was a star performer. He was already a hero in French Canada, and in Montreal he became a hero of epic proportions. His ability and leadership were major factors in Montreal's ten first place finishes and ten Stanley Cup victories during his career.

Beliveau learned to skate on a rink in the back yard of his Victoriaville home. When he was still in his early teens, he was playing hockey in a men's league. He quickly progressed to Junior A hockey with the Quebec City Citadels. Soon he became the outstanding professional prospect in Canada and Quebec City's greatest hero. In his final junior season Beliveau scored 61 goals and 124 points in 43 games.

The Montreal Canadiens' fans eagerly awaited his arrival in the NHL. When he was a junior in

Quebec City, the modern 15,000 seat Quebec Coliseum had been completed and the building was sometimes called "The House That Jean Built." The Coliseum had been packed with spectators for every junior game in which Beliveau played. But when he was too old for junior hockey, Beliveau surprised the fans in Montreal. He decided to stay and

Jean Beliveau (left).

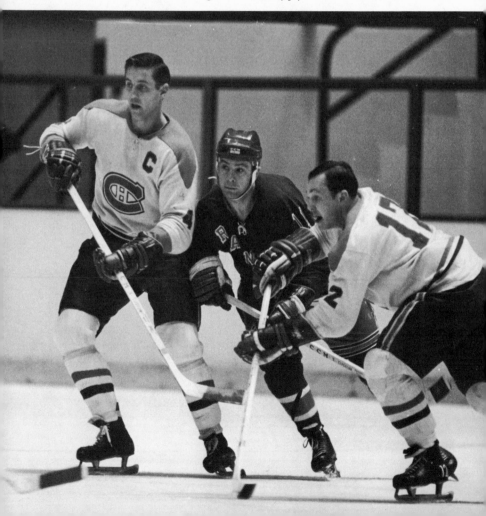

play with the Quebec City Aces, a senior amateur team. He turned down the lucrative NHL contract offered by the Canadiens.

The big center excelled in the Quebec League and the Aces attracted capacity crowds. In answer to the impatient fans in Montreal, Beliveau explained, "I wanted to play in the NHL with the Canadiens, of course. But I felt I had an obligation to the fans in Quebec City who had done so much for me."

Finally, in 1953 the Canadiens were able to get Beliveau's signature on an NHL contract. Montreal was building perhaps the strongest team in NHL history and Beliveau became the big, strong center the club had lacked. The Canadiens' line-up was loaded with superstar players—goalie Jacques Plante, defensemen Doug Harvey and Tom Johnson, forwards Maurice Richard, Dickie Moore and Boom-Boom Geoffrion.

An effortless skater, brilliant scorer and playmaker, and sufficiently combative to discourage harassment from opposing players, Beliveau quickly became a major star. In his rookie season he played in only 44 games because of injuries, scoring 13 goals and 21 assists. But in 1954–55 he scored 37 goals and 36 assists and earned a place on the First All-Star Team. The next season the Canadiens began a streak of five consecutive Stanley Cup triumphs with Beliveau the leader, both on and off the ice.

Big Jean slumped in the early 1960s due to injuries, but in 1964–65 he was the leader of a new Canadien powerhouse which included young stars Yvan Cournoyer, John Ferguson, Jacques Laperriere and J. C. Tremblay. Montreal won the Stanley Cup four times in the next five seasons.

In 1967–68 Beliveau demonstrated his importance to the Canadiens. He missed most of the season's first half due to injuries, and when he rejoined the team late in December, the Canadiens were in last place. Led by their great center, Montreal fought their way back to first place and then won the Stanley Cup. Winning the Cup meant more to Beliveau than earning the extra money. "Money is not the main incentive for the Canadiens," he said. "The Stanley Cup is important to us. We feel we represent French-Canada and winning the Cup for our supporters is the big objective."

Early in the 1970s Beliveau was completing a career that had been filled with honors. As the decade opened, he was second on the NHL's all-time point list to Gordie Howe. He had won the Hart Trophy as most valuable player twice, the NHL scoring championship once, and had been nominated to the All-Star Team in ten different years.

In contrast to his former teammate Rocket Richard, Beliveau was peaceable and modest. These qualities, along with his remarkable ability, made him one of the most popular players in NHL history.

In 1954 Canadian hockey fans received the biggest jolt of their lives. The Russian National hockey team won the world amateur championship in Stockholm, Sweden, by upsetting Canada 7–2. Up to that point Canada had dominated the world amateur hockey scene just as it had supplied almost all of the players in North American professional hockey. The 1954 Russian victory was a complete surprise because few people realized that the Soviets were playing hockey seriously.

The Stockholm upset was merely an indication of what was to follow. Although Canada won the title four times between 1955 and 1961, the 1960s belonged to Russia on the world hockey ponds. From 1963 to 1971 the powerful Russian teams swept nine consecutive global titles, rolling over the world hockey powers, Canada, Sweden and Czechoslovakia, in an unprecedented domination of the sport.

The Russian approach to hockey was the same as that nation had adopted towards many other endeavors. They decided that hockey was a game at

Eugeny Maiorov (14) scores for the Soviet Union against Canada's goalie in the 1964 world championship match.

which they could excel and that success in world play would provide useful propaganda for the Soviet way of life. Thus, their efforts in hockey were both sporting and political.

Until 1954 Canada had been able to win the world amateur and Olympic Games titles with mediocre teams. In 1954 at Stockholm, Canada was represented by a team from a Toronto commercial league, sponsored by a used car dealer and strengthened by the addition of several top amateurs. The top caliber Canadian skaters played professionally in the world's best league, the National Hockey League, and the three minor pro groups in North America.

The Russians attracted some attention early in the tournament by winning their games against weak opponents. The interest in the Soviet team increased as it rolled undefeated towards the final game against Canada, which was also unbeaten. In the decisive game the Canadians never had a chance. Russia dominated the game from the opening face-off and scored an easy win. The world hockey picture changed instantly.

The Canadian reaction was predictable. In the 1955 tournament Canada was represented by a much stronger team, the Penticton (British Columbia) Vees, a rowdy, hard-hitting club with several former pro players as its stars. The Russians spent much of the final game picking themselves up off the ice where they had been deposited by Canadian bodychecks. Canada won 5–0.

The Russians came back to win the hockey gold medal in the 1956 Olympics, then made their first Canadian tour. They met the best senior amateur teams and won most of their games. The star of the Soviet team was big defenseman Nicolai Sologubov, a happy-looking man who smiled a great deal of the time on the ice and could deliver a bodycheck in the best hockey manner.

Canada sent its strongest teams to the 1958 and 1959 world tournaments and regained the title in close contests against the Russians. Additional strong opposition was provided by Sweden and Czechoslovakia. The United States supplied a major upset at the 1960 Olympic Games in Squaw Valley, California, by winning the gold medal. Canada won its last world title in 1961 and then lost to Sweden in 1962 as the Russians and Czechs boycotted the event for political reasons.

By 1963 the Russians had completed a reconstruction of that first strong team in the 1950s. Coached by Anatoli Tarasov and Arkady Chernyshev, the Russians swept the world championship for the following eight years.

The advancement in the caliber of hockey played by the Russian team was remarkable. In the 1950s their equipment was far behind the gear worn by North American teams, but they quickly upgraded it. In the early years the Soviets used a planned attack with preconceived plays in the manner of North American football. Opposing teams could break down this system by tight checking, especially in the Russian zone. However, the superior Russian physical conditioning, their excellence in hockey fundamentals, and their well-planned strategy led to their unprecedented sweep of the world event.

Three players were the mainstays of all nine world championship teams—220 pound defenseman Alex Ragulin, center Veniamin Alexandrov and goalie Victor Konovalenko. In 1965 the Russians debuted their great winger Anatoli Firsov, who quickly established himself as one of the world's best players. A strong skater with a superb shot and stick-handling ability, Firsov would have been a major star in the NHL.

HOCKEY'S BLACKEST NIGHT

The blackest night in the history of the National Hockey League was touched off by an incident involving tempestuous Maurice "Rocket" Richard, the Montreal Canadiens' hot-tempered, high-scoring right winger.

In Montreal and the entire province of Quebec, hockey is followed with greater intensity than anywhere else in the world. The Canadiens and their players always have been subjects of passionate devotion. Montreal's French-Canadian stars often received the kind of reverent attention usually reserved for a government leader or a religious figure. Of the stars who wore the Montreal uniform, Richard was the most revered of all.

Few athletes in any sport rewarded their fans as richly as Richard. His burning desire to excel as a representative of French-Canada inspired him to unequalled heights, and he was at his best when the cheers of his fans rocked the Montreal Forum. Still, Richard's quick temper and his habit of personally revenging fouls and harassment frequently landed him in trouble. He earned several suspensions and paid many fines during his career.

Entering the 1954–55 season, Richard had won every honor available to an NHL player, except the scoring title. Although he had led the league in goals five times, he had never acquired a sufficient number of assists to claim the total points title.

Richard had an excellent season in 1954–55 with the powerhouse Canadiens. With three games remaining in the schedule, he led the NHL in points by a narrow margin over his young Montreal teammate, Bernie "Boom-Boom" Geoffrion. Richard's adoring fans were certain he would claim the one hockey prize that had eluded him.

Then, in a game at Boston on March 13, 1955, Richard and Bruin defenseman Hal Laycoe became involved in a fight that turned into a wild, stick-swinging fracas. Richard struck Laycoe several times with his stick and punched a linesman who was attempting to restrain him. NHL president Clarence Campbell immediately suspended Richard for the rest of the season and for the Stanley Cup playoffs.

Richard's suspension set off a tremendous furor in Montreal. Campbell received many threatening telephone calls and letters. Fans begged the Canadian government to act on Richard's behalf and have the suspension lifted. One supporter sent a telegram to Queen Elizabeth in England, asking her to help the Rocket.

The Canadiens' first home game following Richard's suspension was on March 17 against the De-

An usher restrains an irate Montreal fan after the fan struck NHL president Campbell (right) on March 17, 1955.

troit Red Wings. Fans gathered in groups outside the Forum in mid-afternoon, and when Campbell arrived at the game with a special police guard, he was greeted by a thunderous boo and pelted with debris.

The game started as scheduled and the first period passed without incident. But when Detroit scored in the second period, the crowd became restless. A young man, wearing a leather windbreaker, approached Campbell and extended his hand. When the NHL president reached to shake the hand, he was punched in the face. Then several other youths tried to attack him. The police had almost restored order when a tear gas bomb exploded on the ice. The crowd rushed for the exits and a panic almost resulted.

The crowd pouring out of the building joined the many fans who had been unable to get inside for the game. Fights broke out, and some windows in the Forum were smashed by rifle shots. The crowd quickly became an uncontrollable mob. The mass of people poured down St. Catherine Street, breaking windows, setting fires and looting stores.

Police and firemen required several hours to bring the mob under control and extinguish the fires. Few buildings in the area of the Forum escaped damage. The police also had a difficult time guiding Campbell out of the Forum and through the angry crowd. Despite the violent reaction, Campbell refused to change Richard's suspension.

Geoffrion finished the season strongly to win the scoring title by one point, 75–74, over Richard. Geoffrion was booed by the Montreal fans because they felt he had deprived their biggest hero of the one honor he had failed to win in his remarkable career.

THE GREAT GOALIES

During the 1950s five goaltenders arrived in the National Hockey League to begin great careers: Terry Sawchuk, Jacques Plante, Lorne "Gump" Worsley, Glenn Hall and Johnny Bower. Each had a unique style of playing the most demanding position in sports. The only thing they had in common was their ability to prevent hockey's best shooters from scoring goals.

These five men won the Vezina Trophy, which is awarded to the goalie(s) on the team allowing the lowest number of goals against, a total of 18 times. Collectively, they earned 27 All-Star Team nominations, including 15 selections to the First Team. They left an indelible mark on the face of hockey.

Amazingly, all five continued their careers far past the age when most professional athletes retire. Bower played his final NHL game during the 1969–70 season when he was 46 years of age. Sawchuk was 41 when he died suddenly in May 1970, and he had planned to continue his career. Plante and Worsley (42) and Hall (39) were still active in 1971.

Five great goalies began their careers in the 1950s: (clockwise from top) Johnny Bower, Lorne "Gump" Worsley, Glenn Hall, Jacques Plante and Terry Sawchuk.

Sawchuk made a smash debut in the NHL with Detroit during the 1950–51 season when he allowed only 1.98 goals per game and had 11 shutouts. He won the Vezina Trophy as the top goalie and the Calder Trophy as the best rookie. He also brought a new style to his craft. Instead of standing erect, Sawchuk crouched, bending at the waist almost in a right angle. "I was able to move more quickly, especially with my legs, because the stance gave me good balance," Sawchuk said. "It also allowed me to have better vision on screened shots from the point."

Sawchuk survived an unbelievable series of injuries and illnesses, including mononucleosis, herniated discs in his back, a collapsed lung, severe eye damage, 400 facial stitches, several broken fingers, cut hand tendons and a broken shoulder. Still, he acquired a record 103 shutouts during his career. He won the Vezina Trophy four times and earned All-Star honors in five seasons.

Plante was the most revolutionary goaltender in NHL history. He contributed two features to the job which most goalies now use. He was the first goalie to wear a protective face mask and the first to wander out of the net to field a loose puck. The Montreal management opposed both moves. They feared that the mask would reduce his vision and that he would be trapped out of his net and scored against. However, all goalies now wear face masks and travel out of the net.

Plante was a superb technician, especially in the

art of "playing the net," positioning himself between the attacker and the goal in a manner that greatly reduced the shooter's available net openings. A seven-time Vezina Trophy winner, Plante achieved a goals against average of 2.37, the lowest of any modern goalie. His playoff figure was 2.08 in 105 games. He retired once after the 1965–66 season but then returned to the NHL, at the age of 39, with St. Louis in 1968–69. He shared the Blues' goaling job and compiled a 1.96 average in 36 games. Plante claimed he never had played more effectively.

An intense, nervous man who was sick to his stomach before every game, Glenn Hall also brought a highly individual style to the NHL. He joined Detroit in 1955–56, then was traded to Chicago two years later. Hall played goal with his legs spread apart in an inverted "Y", and dug the toes of his skates into the ice. He frequently fell to his knees, supposedly a weak position for any goalie, but his lightning reflexes and great catching hand compensated for any style shortcomings.

Hall earned 11 All-Star Team selections and won the Vezina Trophy three times. He was drafted by St. Louis in the 1967 lottery to stock the six NHL expansion teams and was the main reason for the Blues' winning the West Division title in two of their first three seasons.

Bower was 29 years old when he got his first chance to play in the NHL, with New York. Despite his solid rookie year, the Rangers re-assigned him to the minors the following season and he was resigned to finishing his career with Cleveland in the American League. However, Toronto purchased his contract in 1958, and Bower supplied the Maple Leafs with superb goaling for the next dozen years. He anchored four Stanley Cup victories by the Maple Leafs and always was at his best in the big games. Even when he reached his 40s, he displayed the reflexes and agility of a teenager.

Few goalies faced the barrage of shots that were fired at chubby Gump Worsley during his decade with New York. The Rangers were a poor team during the 1950s, but Worsley maintained a respectable goals against average while defending against more than 40 shots in most games.

Worsley possessed a quick wit. During a losing season with New York, Worsley was asked which NHL team gave him the most trouble. Without hesitation, he replied: "The Rangers, of course!"

Worsley finally landed on a winning team when a 1963 trade sent him to Montreal and Plante to New York. He supplied splendid goaltending for four Montreal Stanley Cup winning teams. Late in the 1969–70 season he was traded to the Minnesota North Stars by Montreal. Again his strong work helped his team to earn a playoff berth.

GOLD IN SQUAW VALLEY

Hockey was introduced in the United States soon after it became an important Canadian sport, but the Americans did not produce many star hockey players of their own. Even today the great majority of NHL players were born and raised in Canada. It was 1960 before a team of U.S. players counted an important victory. In that year the U.S. team won the Olympic Games gold medal in hockey in one of the biggest upsets in Olympic history.

Although it is generally accepted that ice hockey first was played in the U.S. in 1893, both Yale University in New Haven and Johns Hopkins University in Baltimore claim to be the site of the first game. The first organized U.S. league was formed in New York in 1896 with four teams: the St. Nicholas Skating Club, the Brooklyn Skating Club, the New York Athletic Club and the Crescent Athletic Club of Brooklyn. By 1902 several leagues flourished in the northeastern section of the country, including the Intercollegiate League with teams from Harvard, Yale, Brown, Princeton and Columbia.

The game became popular at the high school

and college level and in amateur leagues, especially in New England. When hockey was introduced as an Olympic sport in 1920, the U.S. team won the silver medal. Until 1960 the Americans had finished second in five Olympic competitions, third in one. The Canadian team had won the gold medal five times.

The U.S. team received little attention heading into the 1960 Winter Olympics at Squaw Valley, California. The big battle was expected to be between Russia and Canada. The Russians, who had made big strides forward in hockey following their 1954 upset of Canada in the world amateur tournament, had won the Olympic gold medal in 1956 against a strong Canadian team.

The 1960 U.S. team was coached by Jack Riley, who had coached the U.S. Military Academy team at West Point for many years. The U.S. Olympic team drew most of its players from the eastern colleges and from Minnesota. Goalie Jack McCartan, who was to be the most important player in the Olympics, had played college hockey at the University of Minnesota. Other key performers were veteran amateur star Johnny Mayasich, Roger and Billy Christian of Minnesota, Bob and Bill Cleary of Boston, Paul Johnson, and Tommy Williams, who later played with the Boston Bruins and the Minnesota North Stars.

The U.S. team quickly displayed a strong attack by whipping West Germany 9–1 in its first game.

Bill Cleary scored five goals. In the next game the Americans trailed Czechoslovakia 4–3 at the end of the second period and appeared to be running out of steam. Then they received help from a surprising source. Nicolai Sologubov, the great Russian defenseman, told the U.S. team that an oxygen tank was available in one of the dressing rooms. The U.S. players inhaled the oxygen and came back refreshed to score six goals in the third period for a 9–4 victory.

At this point people began to notice the slick-skating, hard-checking U.S. team. Riley had his team playing disciplined positional hockey. Still, few of the 9,000 spectators who jammed the Squaw Valley rink gave the U.S. any chance of winning its first big test. They were scheduled to face the Canadian team, the Kitchener-Waterloo Dutchmen.

Although the Canadians out-played the U.S. team by a big margin, time and time again they were denied goals by McCartan's brilliant goalkeeping. His great saves earned repeated ovations from the partisan crowd, which was caught up in the spirit displayed by the enthusiastic U.S. club. While McCartan kept the goals out, Bob Cleary and Paul Johnson each scored to give the U.S. a 2–0 lead in the first two periods. Canada scored in the third, but couldn't beat McCartan again. The final score was 2–1. The U.S. goalie, who went on to a professional hockey career, made 39 stops.

Two days later the U.S. team faced its second

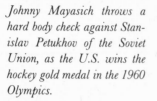

Johnny Mayasich throws a hard body check against Stanislav Petukhov of the Soviet Union, as the U.S. wins the hockey gold medal in the 1960 Olympics.

formidable foe in the powerful Russian National team. Despite their surprising victory over Canada, the Americans were underdogs again. "The experts just wouldn't believe that our team was that good," said Tommy Williams. "They figured our win over Canada was a fluke. But they didn't take into consideration the great spirit and desire we had. Every player on our team was a strong skater. Maybe we lacked a little in finesse, but we made up for it in ambition."

The experts appeared to be correct when the poised Russians took a 2–0 lead early in the game. But the never-say-die attitude of the American club and the enthusiastic backing of their fans inspired the U.S. players to battle back for a 3–2 victory and the Olympic Games gold medal. At the end of the game the U.S. team swarmed onto the ice, slapping each other's back and shouting. The U.S. had gained its first big hockey victory.

THE GOLDEN JET
AND THE HAWKS

In the dozen seasons following World War II most National Hockey League teams enjoyed a period of great prosperity. However, prosperity completely eluded the Chicago Black Hawks. Black Hawk teams were often the worst in the league and reached the Stanley Cup playoffs only once between 1946 and 1958. Several times in that period the Black Hawks were in danger of going out of business altogether, but financial and player aid from the other five clubs saved the team.

In 1954 Tommy Ivan, who had coached the Detroit Red Wings with great success, joined the Hawks as general manager, and the Chicago scene brightened. Ivan's first chore was to build a strong farm system. The previous Hawk management had relied on the purchase of players from other teams to stock the club. Ivan realized that success in the NHL could be achieved only when the Hawks had a strong player development program of their own. Bob Wilson became Chicago's chief scout and he discovered several players who were to restore the Hawks to the NHL's front ranks.

Bobby Hull.

Wilson's most important discovery was a solidly-built, blond-haired youngster named Bobby Hull. Wilson first saw Hull in a boys' game in Hull's tiny hometown of Point Anne in eastern Ontario. The scout convinced Hull's parents that they should permit the boy to leave home and join the junior team in Hespeler, Ontario, which the Hawks sponsored. Hull moved to Hespeler and from there he progressed to Junior A hockey in St. Catharines, where the Hawks developed many of the stars who were to carry them back to the NHL spotlight.

By the time he reached 18 years of age, Bobby Hull was ready to lead the Black Hawks. Hull joined the Hawks for the 1957–58 season and launched one of the NHL's most distinguished careers. Nicknamed "The Golden Jet," Hull quickly crashed the superstar ranks and became the NHL's top player of the 1960s.

Through Ivan's smart dealing and the strong farm system, the parts began to fall into place to give the Hawks a contending team. Goalie Glenn Hall was acquired from Detroit in a 1957 trade. Defensemen Pierre Pilote and Elmer Vasko, forwards Hull, Ken Wharram and Ab McDonald came out of the Hawks' farm system. Further trades brought in defensemen Al Arbour and Dollard St. Laurent, forwards Ron Murphy, Ed Litzenberger, Bill Hay, Eric Nesterenko and Murray Balfour.

Rudy Pilous, who had masterminded the St. Catharines junior team, became the Chicago coach in 1957, and in 1959 combative little center Stan Mikita joined the team directly from junior hockey. The Black Hawks now were ready to challenge the whole league.

Chicago finished in third place during the 1960–61 season, 17 points behind the first-place Montreal Canadiens, who had been Stanley Cup champions for five consecutive seasons. The new Black Hawks were led by the "Million Dollar Line" of Hay, Hull and Balfour, by the sound defensive work of Arbour, Pilote and Vasko, and by Hall's superb goaling. Facing the Canadiens in the Stanley Cup semi-finals, the Black Hawks were given little chance. But backed by Glenn Hall's excellent goal work, the Hawks checked the powerful Montreal attack to a standstill and won the series in six games.

Hall blanked the Canadiens 3–0 in each of the last two games.

Chicago continued its strong defensive work in the Stanley Cup final against the Detroit Red Wings. The Hawks won the series in six games. After the teams divided the first four games, Chicago's superior scoring power carried it to 6–3 and 5–1 wins in the final two games.

The Stanley Cup victory was the Black Hawks' first since the 1937–38 season and it launched Chicago on a decade of great prosperity. The Hawks were unable to repeat the Cup victory although they did finish in first place for the first time in their history during the 1966–67 season. In 1968–69, they fell all the way to last place, then made an amazing comeback, finishing first in 1969–70.

In 1970–71 the Black Hawks were shifted to the West Divison, made up mostly of new expansion teams. They finished first in the division, then fought their way into the Stanley Cup finals. The series, against Montreal, went to seven games. The Hawks lost the finale, missing the Cup once again.

A PUNCH IN TORONTO

In the early 1960s the Toronto Maple Leafs regained their winning ways. The story of their success was largely the story of "Punch" Imlach, their caustic manager-coach. When Imlach, who never played a game in the National Hockey League, assumed command of the Maple Leafs in 1958, the club was in a prolonged slump. The Leafs had finished out of the playoffs for two seasons. Although the club owned some promising young players, the road back to prominence appeared to be all uphill.

In three years the development of that young talent plus Imlach's shrewd deals built the team into a powerhouse. The Leafs were not a classic hockey machine with an overpowering offense. They had a superb goalie in Johnny Bower, great physical strength, and the defensive ability to win on a minimum of offensive output. And they had depth—a good combination of young legs and old heads. Although several teams had more individual stars than the Leafs, no club had as many solid big league hockey players.

Imlach had been a senior amateur player in Toronto and had played with the Canadian Army team during the war years. In one senior game he was hit and stunned by a high stick and the injury had affected his balance. Someone mentioned that Imlach looked "punchy" and the nickname stuck. After returning from the Armed Services, Imlach spent 11 years as a player, coach, manager and part-owner of the Quebec Aces in the Quebec Senior League, and three years as manager-coach of the Springfield team in the American League before accepting the Toronto post.

One of the Leafs' mainstays was goalie Johnny Bower, although he was 35 years of age at the time. Imlach often called Bower "the world's most amazing athlete."

"Bower's birthdate is listed as 1924, but I think he's older than that," Imlach said. "For him to play goal in the NHL, the most demanding job in professional sports, when he's in his 40s, and be the best in the league has to make him a truly great athlete."

Imlach made deals for two veterans—defenseman Allan Stanley and winger Bert Olmstead—who joined the Leafs' experienced players, Tim Horton, Ron Stewart and George Armstrong, to give a solid nucleus of veterans. The Leaf farm system contributed defensemen Bob Baun and Carl Brewer, forwards Billy Harris, Bob Pulford, Bob Nevin, Dick Duff, Frank Mahovlich and Dave Keon. Later, Imlach added center Red Kelly, who teamed with Mahovlich to give the Leafs the required scoring punch.

Frank Mahovlich gave scoring punch to Punch Imlach's Toronto teams and later became a star with the Canadiens.

Not a great teacher of hockey's basic skills, Imlach had a system that developed sound conditioning, solid checking and stamina. The Leaf workouts were the longest and most strenuous in the NHL. Some of Imlach's ploys to inspire his team became hockey folklore. One season when the Leafs were losing a game that could wrap up a playoff berth, Imlach had the box office of Maple Leaf Gardens deliver $30,000 in small bills to the dressing room after the second period. He dumped the money in the middle of the floor to show the players how much bonus money they would lose if they missed the playoffs. The Leafs rallied to win the game.

The Leafs had matured into a championship club by the 1961–62 season. They finished second to

Montreal during the regular schedule, then eliminated the New York Rangers in the semi-finals.
Then they met the Chicago Black Hawks, who had
eliminated the Canadiens, in the final. The Leafs
won in six games to claim their first Stanley Cup
since 1951. The team's victory parade through the
streets of downtown Toronto attracted more than
100,000 people.

The Leafs finished in first place during the
1962–63 season following a hectic, schedule-long
battle with Montreal, Detroit and Chicago. They
swept to the Cup by eliminating Montreal and Detroit in five games apiece. Imlach was at his abrasive
best during the tight race, encouraging, berating
and bullying the Leafs into first place. He had a
feud with the Toronto press halfway through the
season when he banned the writers from the dressing
room for 30 minutes after the games. One Toronto
newspaper didn't mention Imlach's name for half
the season.

The Leafs lurched through the 1963–64 season,
losing 13 games in a row at one point. However, Imlach swung a late season deal to keep the team's
Cup-winning streak alive. He secured veterans
Andy Bathgate and Don McKenney from New
York in exchange for five players. The two new
players provided the impetus the Leafs needed.

Toronto rallied late in the season to finish third
and qualify for the playoffs. The 1964 Stanley Cup
playoffs produced as much excitement as any in his-

tory. Each series required the maximum seven games. The Leafs fell behind Montreal three games to two, but then won two in a row behind Bower's brilliant goaltending, 3–0 and 3–1. Then they met Detroit in the final. Once again Toronto fell behind three games to two. In the sixth game Leaf defenseman Bob Baun, playing with a broken bone in his ankle, scored the winning goal in overtime. Toronto won its third consecutive Stanley Cup with a 4–0 victory in the deciding game.

The Toronto streak ended the following season, but Punch Imlach and his Maple Leafs had earned an important place in hockey history.

THE MILESTONE GOALS

When Maurice "Rocket" Richard, the superb right winger of the Montreal Canadiens, retired following the 1959–60 season, he held two remarkable records. Richard had scored 544 goals during his career, and during the 1944–45 season he had established the single-season standard by making 50 goals in 50 games.

During the 1960s two of the game's great stars— Gordie Howe and Bobby Hull—took aim at these records and finally broke them with perhaps the two most famous goals in hockey history. The two milestone goals had much in common. Both Howe and Hull were being followed by a legion of reporters, commentators and television cameras as they neared their record goals. And both suffered through several scoreless games, increasing the suspense and excitement, before they finally made their record-breaking goals.

When Richard retired in 1960 with his 544 goals, Howe had a total of 496 goals. The two had been in the league together for 14 years. It was generally agreed that Howe was the finest all-around

The two big record-breakers: Bobby Hull and Gordie Howe.

player the game had ever seen while Richard was
the best goal scorer. Still, Howe scored more goals
than Richard in seven of the 14 seasons and tied him
once.

In the three seasons following Richard's retirement, Howe scored 23, 33, and 38 goals. Thus he
opened the 1963–64 campaign with 540 goals, only
four short of Richard's mark. Big Gordie started out
in high gear, and on October 28, 1963, he tied the
record with a goal against Montreal.

In the following two weeks Howe went through a
mysterious scoring slump. He said he was pressing
too hard instead of playing his normal relaxed style
of hockey. With the cameras recording his every
move, Howe finally got his big goal on November 11
against Richard's old team, the Canadiens. The
puck squirted loose from a scramble and Howe deposited it into the net with a quick flick of his wrists.

Richard's other record—50 goals in one season—
was the subject of hot debate long before it was broken. Richard's fans claimed that the mark could be
equalled only if some player scored 50 goals or more
in 50 games as Rocket did. Others countered that
argument with the claim that Richard had set his
record against weak competition since most of the
good players were in the armed forces (it was during
World War II).

The first assault on Richard's record came in the
1960–61 season when Montreal's Boom-Boom Geoffrion chalked up 50 goals in a 70-game schedule. A

year later Hull also scored 50 goals in 70 games. From the start of the 1965–66 season it was evident that Hull, hockey's "Golden Jet," would challenge Richard's record if he could avoid injuries. He scored 11 times in his first six games, and after 23 games he had 27 goals. But late in the season Hull missed five games with injuries. He just missed equalling the one goal per game standard, scoring his 50th goal in his 52nd game of the season. Still, it was clear that Hull would be the first to score more than 50 goals in any season and that he would set a new season record.

An enormous group of newsmen and photographers were following Hull's every move, waiting for Number 51. The pressure of the situation built to a nerve-wracking peak that seemed to affect the entire Chicago club. Following Hull's record-tying score, the Hawks were blanked three straight times by Toronto, Montreal and New York. Every time Hull touched the puck, the fans were on their feet.

"Sometimes we wondered if Hull or any other Chicago player, for that matter, would ever score again," said one of Hull's mates.

On March 12 in a game at Chicago Stadium against the New York Rangers, a crowd of more than 20,000 spectators was jammed into every available inch of space. The game was scoreless through the first period. Then Hull's linemate Chico Maki slapped in Chicago's first goal in four games.

"Chico's was the biggest goal of the season,"

Hull said. "When he scored, everyone relaxed a little."

Three minutes later Hull fielded a loose puck near the Chicago blueline and raced across center ice, his sweater flapping behind him. As he neared the New York blueline, Ranger defenseman Jim Neilson moved out to check him. Hull wound up for a slapshot, but struck the puck with the heel of his stick. The shot was low, but not especially fast. Hull figured that Ranger goalie Cesare Maniago would stop the puck easily. But Chicago winger Eric Nesterenko sped in front of the Ranger net, distracting Maniago. The Ranger goalie took his eye off the puck and it went past him into the net.

The delirious Chicago fans greeted the goal with a tremendous ovation that lasted 20 minutes. Hull had to leave the bench several times to acknowledge the cheers. Hull scored 54 goals by season's end and made 52 in the following campaign. In 1968–69 he broke his own record by scoring 58 goals in 76 games.

THE
REFORMATION
OF MIKITA

In a November 1966 game against the Boston Bruins, Stan Mikita, the great center of the Chicago Black Hawks, sat in the penalty box and made the most important decision of his hockey career.

"We had a 3–2 lead at the time and I took a stupid penalty for roughing," Mikita recalled. "I worried that the penalty might cost us the lead and the game. Right then, I decided that I had to stay out of the penalty box. One season I served 154 minutes in penalties. You don't score many goals and assists when you're sitting out that much time. You need a very long stick to score goals from the penalty bench."

Mikita's decision came as a complete surprise to his opponents. In his career in Canadian junior hockey and his early years in the NHL, Mikita acquired a reputation as a tough, aggressive player who retaliated instantly whenever he was fouled.

"As a scorer, a player is the target for elbows and sticks," Mikita said. "In my early NHL seasons, when I was fouled, I handed it back immediately when the fans and officials were watching me. I de-

Stan Mikita crashes into an opposing goalie.

cided on a legal, and later, approach to retaliation. When a player fouled me, I'd wait a few games, catch him with his head down and give him a legal check."

Mikita's reformation led to his winning three major individual awards in one season, the first time in NHL history a player had accomplished that feat. During the 1966–67 season he won the Art Ross Trophy as leading scorer, the Hart Trophy as most valuable player, and the Lady Byng Trophy as the most gentlemanly and effective player.

His new approach to the game merely improved a splendid hockey player. During the 1960s he was the most honored performer in the National Hockey League. Mikita earned six First Team and two Second Team All-Star selections, was the leading scorer four times, won the Hart Trophy as the NHL's most valuable player twice. After 1966 he was a two-time winner of the Lady Byng Trophy which is awarded to the player who combines gentlemanly conduct and a high standard of playing ability.

Mikita's reformation was not the first sudden change in his life. He was born on a small farm near Sokolov, Czechoslovakia. When he was eight years old, his aunt and uncle were visiting from their home in St. Catharines, Ontario. Mikita's parents gave him the choice of returning to Canada with his relatives or remaining in the poverty conditions there. He decided to migrate to Canada.

"Letting me go was a terribly difficult decision

for my parents to make, but they realized that I would have the chance for a better life in Canada," Mikita recalled. "On the train out of Czechoslovakia, I cried, and plotted how I could get off it."

When he arrived in St. Catharines, he spoke no English. For several weeks he was afraid to go outdoors. But when he saw some boys playing hockey on the street with a ball, he joined them. The first English words he learned were hockey terms.

"Of course, a few kids made fun of me because I couldn't speak the language," he said. "They called me D.P., the short form for 'displaced person.' I didn't know what they were saying but I knew it was nasty. I soon had a chip on my shoulder."

Mikita quickly mastered the language and excelled in several sports. His rapid progress in hockey led to a berth with the St. Catharines team in the fast Ontario Junior A league, where many NHL players were developed. Mikita became the league's leading scorer and busiest fighter, although he was only 5-foot-9 and 165 pounds.

Mikita jumped directly from teenage hockey to the Chicago Black Hawks. His aggressiveness led to 119 penalty minutes in his rookie season. "I was small and the big guys in the NHL tried to scare me," he said. "I learned to hand it right back with my stick, my elbows, or my fists if necessary."

From eight goals in his rookie season, Mikita progressed to 19 and 25 goals in his next two seasons. In the 1963–64 season he had 39 goals and 89 points to win his first scoring title. By the end of the 1969–70 season he had averages of .678 assists and 1.108 points per game, the best career marks in NHL history. He was a swift, agile skater and an excellent stickhandler, and he had the ability both to score goals and arrange them for his mates. In addition, he had great defensive talent. He was the complete hockey player, skilled at every facet of the game.

THE AMAZING BOBBY ORR

A favorite joke around the National Hockey League claims that the Boston Bruins began their rebuilding program (which culminated in their 1970 Stanley Cup victory) on March 28, 1948, the day Bobby Orr was born. The joke pointed to something serious—the importance Orr had assumed to the Bruins and the entire NHL.

Orr joined the Bruins in 1966 when he was 18 years old. He was the most publicized rookie in the history of the league and was a superstar from the very beginning. In his first four big league seasons Orr earned every award available to an NHL player and became the highest paid player in hockey. He was already being called the greatest player in the game's history. His incredible play made him the NHL's premier gate attraction. Like Eddie Shore, who was also a Bruin defenseman, Bobby brought out huge crowds of new hockey fans in new NHL cities and brought new attention to the game.

"I watch Orr in every game and I tell myself that's the greatest game of hockey a player ever played," said the Bruins' general manager, Milt

Schmidt. "But in the next game, he seems to be even better. We have yet to find anything that he can't do."

Orr was the perfect athlete. He stood 5-foot-11 and weighed 180 pounds. He was a superb skater with great speed and balance and a hard, accurate shot. He had brilliant stickhandling and playmaking ability and the ability to anticipate what will happen next on the ice. His charm made him an immensely popular player off the ice as well.

Bobby Orr clears the puck for Boston.

Orr first attracted the attention of NHL scouts when he was 12 years old, playing boys' hockey in Parry Sound. At 13, he was a regular defenseman with the Oshawa Generals, a Boston farm team in the fast Ontario Junior A league. Playing against boys up to 20 years old, Orr earned all-star status in his first season. During the 1963–64 season, at 14, he established new junior league scoring records.

Already he was making news and appearing in magazine and newspaper stories. Orr claimed that he never read any of the stories written about him. "I was afraid to read any of the stuff," Orr explained, "because so many people had warned me not to get a swelled head."

In each of his four junior seasons Orr set new records. In Boston, the Bruins were in the middle of a long string of basement finishes. But they told their fans, "Just wait until Bobby Orr gets here."

When he turned 18, Orr was ready for Boston. After a lengthy contract negotiation, he signed the largest pact ever given to an NHL rookie. The Boston team was rebuilding and Orr was the key to their plans. From the time he played his first NHL game, the rabid Bruin fans, who had suffered with their mediocre team for years, immediately fell in love with him.

He acquired all-star status in his first season and never looked back. In the 1967–68 season he established new goal and point standards for defensemen with 21 goals and 43 assists.

However, the best of Orr was yet to come. In 1969–70 he had the greatest season of any player in NHL history, compiling a list of achievements that fill a book and leading the Bruins to their first Stanley Cup in 29 years. He won the scoring title with 120 points, an accomplishment which no defenseman in history had even approached. His astounding scoring ability caused his brilliant defensive play to be overlooked. He collected a total of $17,750 in league bonuses for his individual and team accomplishments and won almost every North American award as athlete of the year, including the Sportsman-of-the-Year award from *Sports Illustrated* magazine.

Despite his unbelievable accomplishments and the accompanying financial rewards, Orr remained a likeable, easy-going, witty young man. Stories of his unpublicized visits to hospitals and crippled children's homes are legendary in hockey's inner circles.

"I'm lucky, right?" Orr said. "I've been gifted. But the world is full of people who not only haven't been gifted, but have had some things taken away from them. All I have to do is see one of them, some little girl who can't walk, and then I don't think I'm such a hero anymore. I think that compared to one of them, I'm a very small article."

IT'S AN OLD MAN'S GAME

Of all the "unlikely" teams to win the Stanley Cup, the leader must be the 1966–67 Toronto Maple Leafs. That season, the Leafs had only two players who scored 20 or more goals. The Detroit Red Wings had five such players, and the Chicago Black Hawks had six. The Leafs used five different goaltenders during the season. Manager-coach George "Punch" Imlach was hospitalized for three weeks and only two players escaped the injury jinx to participate in all 70 games.

Following their three consecutive Cup triumphs between 1962 and 1964, the Leafs had sagged badly. Several players from those teams retired or were traded away as Imlach tried to rebuild the club into a contender. In one puzzling trade, Imlach acquired two aging veterans, goalie Terry Sawchuk and defenseman Marcel Pronovost, from Detroit. They were hardly the type of players to bolster a team that was supposedly rebuilding.

In 1966–67 the Maple Leafs faced trouble from the beginning. Almost every member of the club missed games with injuries. Several times the team appeared to be in imminent danger of dropping out of playoff contention, especially during a ten-game losing streak in January. After the Leafs won a game to end their skid, Imlach was rushed to the hospital where he spent three weeks recovering from a hiatus hernia. Assistant manager Frank "King" Clancy coached the team during Imlach's absence and the Leafs won nine of 12 games.

The Leafs had their worst trouble at the goalie position. Their regular goalies, Johnny Bower, 43, and Terry Sawchuk, 38, spent almost as much time on the injured list as they did in the nets during the season. Before the 1966–67 schedule opened, Sawchuk had had surgery on his back to correct a disc problem that caused him to have a stooped posture. The operation permitted him to stand erect and added two inches to his height. However, in early December he was hospitalized with more back problems and additional surgery was required. He played in only 28 games while Bower's assorted injuries allowed him to play in only 27 contests. Bruce Gamble, Al Smith and Gary Smith were recruited from the farm teams to fill in.

The regular season had been dominated by Chicago, led by superstars Bobby Hull and Stan Mikita. The Black Hawks finished in first place for the first time in their history, far ahead of second-place Montreal. Toronto struggled to third place, only three points ahead of the New York Rangers.

The Leafs managed to hit the playoffs with a

healthy roster. Still, the Leafs were a collection of old men in what is supposed to be a young man's game. Ten of their 19 men on the playoff roster were over 35. Their defense consisted of Pronovost, 36, Allan Stanley, 41, and Tim Horton, 37, plus two relative youngsters, Bob Baun, 31, and Larry Hillman, 30. Two key forwards were Red Kelly, 40, and George Armstrong, 37. It appeared that the strain of the playoffs would be too much for their old legs.

Toronto faced the powerhouse Black Hawks in the semi-final series. It hardly seemed fair to send the old men against a team that featured Mikita, the NHL scoring champ with a record 97 points, Hull (52 goals) and the league-leading goalie tandem of Glenn Hall and Denis DeJordy. However, no one told the old Leafs they weren't supposed to win.

Chicago won the opener easily, 5–2. But in the second game center Dave Keon did a masterful job of checking Mikita, and Sawchuk performed miracles at goal as the Leafs won 3–1. The teams divided the next two games at Toronto.

In the fifth game, at Chicago, Bower got away to a shaky start and was replaced after the first period by Sawchuk. On the Hawks' first rush of the period, a Hull slapper struck Sawchuk on the shoulder, but he continued in the game. The aging goalie faced 38 Chicago shots in 40 minutes of hockey and staged what many experts called the finest exhibition of goaltending in the history of the games as the Leafs won 4–2.

Terry Sawchuk, the hero of the 1966–67 Maple Leafs.

Sawchuk had made several incredible stops of shots by Bobby Hull, and Hull complained after the game, "It was the only time I ever scored five goals and none of them counted."

Toronto wrapped up the series in the sixth game. Rookie Brian Conacher scored two goals and the Leafs won 3–1.

The Maple Leafs faced Montreal in the Cup final and once again they were the underdog. But Sawchuk and Bower played magnificently in goal, and the veteran defensemen operated at peak efficiency. The line of Peter Stemkowski, Jim Pappin and Bob Pulford supplied key goals, and the Leafs won the Stanley Cup in six games.

"Maybe the so-called experts didn't think we'd win," Imlach said. "But my old guys were tough when it counted, and isn't that the mark of a true champion?"

DOUBLE OR NOTHING

For awhile during the 1960s it seemed as if hockey was standing still. The major leagues in North America's other important team sports—football, baseball and basketball—had been expanding slowly, adding one or two teams every few years and bringing major league competition to new areas of the continent. In the meantime, the National Hockey League still had the same six teams and was restricted to eastern Canada and the northeast United States.

But the NHL was planning the most ambitious expansion in professional sports. In February of 1966 the league announced that beginning with the 1967–68 season there would be six additional clubs in the league: the St. Louis Blues, the Minnesota North Stars, the Oakland Seals, the Pittsburgh Penguins, the Philadelphia Flyers and the Los Angeles Kings. These new teams would be allowed to draft a certain number of players from the existing clubs and would form the new NHL West Division. The East Division was made up of the established teams: Toronto, Montreal, Chicago, Detroit, Boston and New York.

Goalie Denis DeJordy (30) and Larry Cahan (3) of the Los Angeles Kings in the new West Division wrestle with a Toronto Maple Leaf.

The older NHL teams had been remarkably successful during the late 1950s and the 1960s. In fact, an empty seat at a big league hockey game was a rarity. In 1963–64 the NHL games were viewed by 95 per cent capacity crowds. But the NHL had not been as successful with television. Televised hockey in Canada was the top program in the ratings, but the NHL had little success in selling its product to the big United States networks. Since there were NHL teams in only four U.S. cities, most sports fans were not very interested in the game. The addition of six new U.S. teams, four of them west of the Mississippi, spread hockey interest throughout the country.

The new team owners, who paid $2,000,000 each for their franchises, were allowed to claim 20 NHL players apiece in the expansion draft. Each of the established clubs was permitted to protect its better players, so the new teams received mostly untried rookies, veterans near the end of their careers, and minor leaguers. Two clubs—Philadelphia and Los Angeles—bought the Quebec and Springfield minor league teams, securing additional players to augment those they acquired in the draft. In the first season Philadelphia and Los Angeles finished in first and second place in the West Division and several players from their minor league purchases were key performers.

The NHL schedule was increased from 70 to 74 games, and the expansion teams were scheduled to play 24 games against established clubs and 50 against other expansion teams. Hockey experts predicted that the talent-poor expansion teams would be no match for the established East Division. But the new teams did better than expected. They collected 33 per cent of the available points in games against the East Division, picking up 40 wins and 18 ties in 144 inter-divisional matches. The defending Stanley Cup champions, the Toronto Maple Leafs, actually lost more games than they won against West Division teams. Although the new clubs still had room for improvement, their first year was judged to be a great success.

The NHL's expansion program proved to be a wise move. Hockey interest was greatly increased in many areas of the United States and countless new fans were introduced to the game. Television coverage was increased, bringing still more interest and more money to the teams. For hockey players the expansion greatly increased their opportunities for a career on ice. Several players who had failed to crack the roster in the old six-team league became stars of the new division.

The St. Louis Blues soon became the most successful of the six new NHL teams. Although they
finished third in the West Division during their first
year, they won the West Division playoffs. In the
next two years they won first place and the division
playoffs as well.

In 1966 the St. Louis application for an NHL
franchise had been given little chance of success.
Minor league professional hockey had failed there
and the hockey arena was in a rundown condition.
However, the Salomons, Sidney, Jr., and his son Sidney Salomon III, made a convincing sales pitch for
St. Louis and the NHL accepted the bid. More than
$2,000,000 was spent to refurbish the arena and
bring it up to NHL standards. When the reconstruction was completed, it was one of the best in the
NHL.

Scotty Bowman, the Blues' brilliant manager-
coach, was first hired as assistant to general manager-coach Lynn Patrick, but he moved up to the
coaching position early in the 1967–68 season. The
Blues got away to a bad start in their first season.

But then Bowman engineered some excellent trades. Most important of these was the acquisition of Gordon "Red" Berenson, who quickly became the Blues' leader. Berenson was a center who had been seeking a chance to play regularly to show what he could do. His earlier trials with Montreal and New York had been disappointing.

Bowman also secured Doug Harvey and Dickie Moore, two players who had been big stars with the Montreal Canadiens in the late 1950s. "Players like Harvey and Moore were accustomed to winning," Bowman said. "That rubs off on the young players like we had. Moore would be worth having on the team if he never scored a goal, just because of the influence he had on the kids."

With their newly-acquired players the Blues started to move. By the end of the season they had climbed to third place in the West Division and had qualified for the Stanley Cup playoffs. St. Louis met the first-place Philadelphia Flyers in the opening playoff round. They seemed on the way to an easy victory when they won three of the first four games. Then the Flyers won the next two. But the Blues held on, winning the seventh game 3–1.

The divisional final pitted the Blues against the Minnesota North Stars in another tight, frantic scramble. Four of the seven games were tied at the end of regulation time and went into overtime. The Blues won three of these contests, including the seventh game, which was in its second overtime period before Ron Shock scored to win for the Blues.

When the Stanley Cup final opened in St. Louis, the East Division champions, the Canadiens, were confident and well rested. They had eliminated Boston and Chicago in only nine games. Montreal had scoring power, speed, poise and experience. Their roster was filled with stars such as Jean Beliveau, Gump Worsley, J. C. Tremblay, Henri Richard and others. By contrast, the Blues had mostly untried young players and aging veterans. And after their hectic series against Minnesota, the Blues were tired.

Glenn Hall protects the goal as the St. Louis Blues play Montreal in the 1969 Stanley Cup finals.

However, backed by Hall's superior goaltending, the tight-checking Blues had a big surprise in store for the Canadiens. In the first game the St. Louis players fought like tigers to hold off the vaunted Montreal offense and Hall supplied a series of unbelievable stops as the teams fought to a 2–2 tie in regulation time. At 1:41 of the first overtime period, Montreal's Jacques Lemaire bombed a thundering slapshot past Hall for the winning goal.

Most experts expected the Blues to fold in front of the Canadien power in the second game. Hall was even better, holding the Canadiens to a single goal, but the Blues were unable to score. Although they had won two in a row, the Montreal players had become believers in the Blues' capabilities. Said one Canadien player, "There were times in that series when we were trying to get a puck past Hall when we asked each other, 'Will we ever beat this guy?' "

Montreal claimed 4–3 and 3–2 wins to wrap up the Stanley Cup in four consecutive games, but St. Louis earned great respect for their plucky display. Even those who had opposed NHL expansion had to admit that the new teams had made a fine showing in their first season.

During the four games of the final playoffs, goalie Hall had faced a total of 151 shots and permitted only 11 goals. In 18 playoff games, he had allowed only 45 scores. His great play earned him the Conn Smythe Trophy as the most valuable player in the playoffs.

THE GREATEST COACH

While the Montreal Canadiens were staging a loud celebration in their dressing room following their Stanley Cup victory over the St. Louis Blues, their coach, Hector "Toe" Blake, stood in the corridor outside the room and announced to a large group of reporters that he was retiring from the job.

Thus the distinguished career of one of the National Hockey League's most remarkable men ended after 26 seasons as a player and coach. The Canadiens had been the league's most successful team, finishing in first place in 19 seasons and winning the Stanley Cup 16 times. Blake had had much to do with these records. During his 13 seasons as a player for the Canadiens, Blake had won many individual honors and was a member of two Cup winning teams and five first-place finishers. As a coach, Blake achieved unprecedented results. In 13 seasons he guided his team to nine first-place finishes and eight Stanley Cup victories, including one streak of five Stanley Cup wins in a row. Only Toronto's Clarence "Hap" Day, who coached five Stanley Cup winners, approached Blake's standard.

The Canadiens' Toe Blake.

As a player, left winger Blake had not been a good natural skater but his considerable desire made him a top NHL star. He scored 235 goals and 292 assists in 572 games, and won the NHL scoring title and most valuable player award in 1938–39. Four times he won the Lady Byng Trophy as the most gentlemanly and effective player. During part of his 13-season career he played on Montreal's famous "Punch Line" with Maurice "Rocket" Richard and Elmer Lach, two hot-headed competitors who benefited from Blake's steadying influence. Blake's career ended in 1948 when he broke an ankle.

After coaching in the minor leagues for several years, Blake was hired for the Montreal post in 1955 to replace Dick Irvin, under whom Blake had played. "We could hire a dozen men who could spout fancy theories about how hockey should be played," said Montreal manager Frank Selke when Blake was hired. "Toe Blake might not talk fancy, but he's the best at making players produce."

The Canadiens had a roster of great players when Blake took command—goalie Jacques Plante, defensemen Doug Harvey and Tom Johnson, forwards Henri and Rocket Richard, Beliveau, Dickie Moore and Bernie Geoffrion. Blake quickly established himself as boss and the team promptly won the Stanley Cup five years in a row.

Blake had many strong players on his teams, but his own abrasive, hard-driving style molded them into a unit. "Toe Blake has been the tremendous force that has driven us to our success," commented Montreal's great center Jean Beliveau when he heard that Blake had retired. "Every player has great respect and admiration for him. He always made us a better team than we were."

Following the Canadiens' victory in 1959–60, the team fell into a slump. Rocket Richard retired and several others retired or were traded. Then Blake took a new group of talented youngsters produced by Montreal's strong farm system plus several players secured in trades and constructed a new Montreal dynasty that won four Stanley Cups in five years between 1965 and 1969.

Despite his remarkable record of achievement, coaching never was an easy vocation for him. A tense, emotional man and a constant worrier, Blake spent many hours walking the streets after games. When the team was playing badly, Blake could be heard shouting at the players in the dressing room between periods.

"Giving it everything I've got is the only approach I know," Blake said. "I often tried the silent treatment on my players but it never worked. My job was to make individuals work together as a unit. I had to drive them hard to accomplish this. Besides, no one ever made it to the top without hard work."

Although he had been a gentlemanly player, Blake's temper frequently exploded at the wrong time when he became a coach. During the 1961 playoffs he was incensed over a penalty call by referee Dalt McArthur. At the game's conclusion he raced across the ice and took a punch at the official. Although he failed to connect with McArthur's chin, Blake was fined $2,000 by the NHL.

In the playoffs two years later, Blake again blew his top at a referee, this time Eddie Powers. He said, "They should investigate officials who handle themselves as if they bet on the games." Blake claimed that his remarks weren't intended for publication, but he was fined again by the league.

On his retirement, Blake was appointed vice-president of the Canadiens. "I missed hockey," he said. "But it was great to be able to sleep at night."

BOBBY AND THE BIG BAD BRUINS

When Bobby Orr scored a goal in overtime against the St. Louis Blues to give the Boston Bruins the 1970 Stanley Cup, a Bruin victory drought of 29 years ended. The big, young, combative Bruins had a star-laden roster, and in the view of most hockey experts, the Bruins' best years were ahead of them.

When the Bruins had won their last Stanley Cup in 1941, they had seemed ready to dominate the NHL for years to come. But then World War II broke up the club as most players entered the armed services. Following the war the Bruins enjoyed some success, but were eclipsed by Detroit and Montreal. Then their fortunes fell to rock bottom. Between the 1959–60 and 1966–67 seasons the Bruins finished out of the playoffs during eight consecutive campaigns.

In 1966–67 Bobby Orr arrived in Boston along with coach Harry Sinden. Orr was an immediate success and Sinden, who was only 31, proved to be the ideal man to handle the young, rollicking club. Still, the Bruins finished last.

A year later Bruin manager Schmidt engineered

a trade that made the Bruins a Stanley Cup contender overnight. Boston secured centers Phil Esposito and Fred Stanfield and winger Ken Hodge from Chicago in exchange for goaltender Jack Norris, defenseman Gil Marotte and center Pit Martin. The deal turned out to be the most lopsided in NHL history. The three new Bruins became important stars with Boston, but only Martin played well with Chicago.

During his seasons with Chicago, Esposito had played center on a line with the Black Hawks' great Bobby Hull. His achievements were dimmed by

Phil Esposito goes in for a shot.

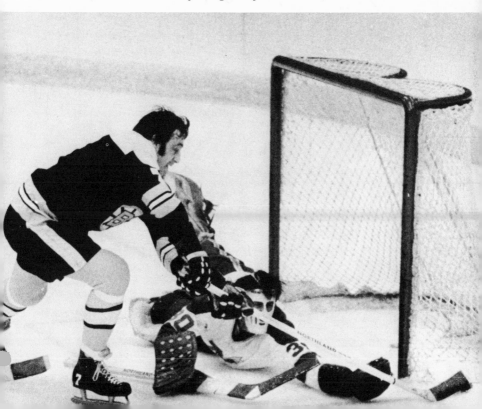

Hull's record scoring feats. With Boston, Esposito became the team leader and the star pivot the Bruins had lacked. Hodge and Stanfield also assumed star roles in Boston, giving the team a lineup of big, strong forwards.

During 1967–68 the Bruins rebounded from a last place standing to third place, earning their first playoff berth since 1958–59. Esposito finished second to Chicago's Stan Mikita in the scoring race, and center Derek Sanderson won the Calder Trophy as the NHL's best rookie. The Bruins were eliminated in four games by the Montreal Canadiens in the first playoff round. But even making the playoffs had been a big step forward for the Bruins.

In 1968–69 the Bruins arrived. Esposito had the greatest season of any scorer in history, gaining 49 goals and 77 assists for 126 points. At the same time Orr established new scoring marks for defensemen. The Bruins finished the season with a club record of 100 points but placed second, three points behind Montreal.

In the playoffs Boston eliminated Toronto with little trouble, outscoring the Leafs 24–5 in winning four straight games. This sent the Bruins against Montreal in the East Division finals and the series was one of the greatest in history. Every game was a thriller. The Canadiens won the series 4–2, but three of their victories were in overtime. The Bruins outscored them 16–15 in the six games.

The 1969–70 season started badly for the Bruins.

In a pre-season game at Ottawa, Ontario, against the St. Louis Blues, Boston's splendid defense veteran Ted Green became involved in a stick-swinging battle with the Blues' Wayne Maki. Green was struck on the head by Maki's stick and fell, unconscious, to the ice. At first doctors believed he had suffered permanent brain damage and would be partially paralyzed. However, he battled back slowly, surviving three operations to insert a steel plate in his head. He returned to the Bruin line-up in 1970–71.

The Bruins' depth of talent permitted them to overcome the loss of their defensive leader. The East Division race was a season-long battle between Chicago, Boston, Detroit, New York and Montreal. Only seven points separated the five clubs at the end of the season. The Bruins and Chicago were tied for the lead with 99 points, but the Black Hawks claimed the pennant because they had more victories than Boston. Orr had an incredible season, winning the point title with 120 and capturing every available individual award. Esposito led the NHL with 43 goals.

The Bruins' toughest playoff opposition came in the opening round against New York. The teams had been bitter rivals during the 1969–70 schedule, and they continued their feud in a tough series which Boston won in six games. The Bruins then defeated Chicago in four games to qualify for the final against St. Louis.

The Bruins simply had too much of everything for the Blues. Boston held a 20–8 margin in goals as they won the Stanley Cup in four games. The top five playoff scorers were Boston players, headed, of course, by Esposito and Orr.

The only close game of the final series was the fourth contest, in which the teams battled to a 3–3 tie during regulation time. The overtime session was a mere 40 seconds old when Orr moved in from the point to accept a pass from Sanderson. He shot the puck into the net, completing his brilliant season with the goal that brought Boston the Cup. The Bruins returned to Boston as conquering heroes. A few days later they rode triumphantly through the city, accepting the congratulations of their thousands of fans.

FROM HERE TO MOSCOW?

In 1970 the National Hockey League staged its second expansion program in a four-year period, adding the Buffalo Sabres and the Vancouver Canucks. Now big league hockey spanned the continent, stretching from Montreal to Vancouver, Boston to California.

Expansion had caused the league to establish a new system of drafting amateur players. This system, similar to that used by the National Football League for American college players, worked in favor of Buffalo and Vancouver, giving the weakest teams first choice in the draft.

The NHL's main source of player talent has long been Canadian junior hockey, where boys between the ages of 16 and 20 years compete under professional conditions. The top junior leagues exist in Western Canada, Ontario and Quebec. The strongest of these is the Ontario Hockey Association Major Junior A Series, the league in which more than 60 per cent of the players in the NHL during 1970–71 served their apprenticeship.

Until 1967 NHL teams sponsored the junior

clubs and stocked them with young players to whom they already had the rights. But this system was abolished in 1967 to give all teams, old and new, a fair chance at promising players. The two new teams, Buffalo and Vancouver, made the first selections in the 1970 draft. Buffalo chose center Gilbert Perreault and Vancouver selected defenseman Dale Tallon. Both Tallon and Perreault were players of exceptional talent.

Another source of potential NHL players was United States college hockey, which made tremendous strides forward during the 1960s. The U.S. colleges recruited many players from Canadian junior hockey by offering athletic scholarships. Several former college players attained success in the NHL,

Gilbert Perrault (11) of the Buffalo Sabres, the NHL's 1971 rookie of the year.

notably Tony Esposito, and Keith Magnuson of the Chicago Black Hawks. The caliber of Canadian college play improved, too, although most young Canadian players preferred to play in the junior leagues.

An exciting prospect for the NHL, and certainly one of the most interesting possibilities in the entire sports world, is a meeting between the NHL champions and the dominant teams in world amateur hockey, Russia and Czechoslovakia. The European teams have so far refused to play against NHL clubs for fear of jeopardizing their Olympic eligibility. But it seems possible that an agreement will eventually be reached to allow such competition.

"A series between the Stanley Cup champions and the Russians is one of the great possibilities in sport for the 1970s," commented NHL president Clarence Campbell. "Such a series could be viewed on worldwide television through the satellite facilities and have an audience that would equal the World Cup in soccer.

"Another fine prospect is having those teams compete for the Stanley Cup. They could have a major league of their own with teams, say, in Russia, Czechoslovakia, Sweden, Germany, Finland and other countries. Then the two winners could meet in a world series of hockey. Perhaps in the 1970s it will happen."

Imagine a Stanley Cup final between the Boston Bruins and the Moscow Selects! Such a meeting would be fitting for the world's fastest sport.

STANLEY CUP WINNERS
PRIOR TO FORMATION OF NATIONAL HOCKEY LEAGUE

1892–93	Montreal A.A.A.	1904–05	Ottawa Silver Seven
1893–94	Montreal A.A.A.	1905–06	Montreal Wanderers
1894–95	Montreal Victorias	1906–07	Kenora Thistles (January)
1895–96	Winnipeg Victorias	1906–07	Montreal Wanderers (March)
	(Feb. 1896)	1907–08	Montreal Wanderers
1895–96	Montreal Victorias	1908–09	Ottawa Senators
	(Dec. 1896)	1909–10	Montreal Wanderers
1896–97	Montreal Victorias	1910–11	Ottawa Senators
1897–98	Montreal Victorias	1911–12	Quebec Bulldogs
1898–99	Montreal Shamrocks	1912–13	Quebec Bulldogs
1899–1900	Montreal Shamrocks	1913–14	Toronto Blueshirts
1900–01	Winnipeg Victorias	1914–15	Vancouver Millionaires
1901–02	Montreal A.A.A.	1915–16	Montreal Canadiens
1902–03	Ottawa Silver Seven	1916–17	Seattle Metropolitans
1903–04	Ottawa Silver Seven		

STANLEY CUP WINNERS
AFTER THE FORMATION OF NATIONAL HOCKEY LEAGUE

1917–18	Toronto Arenas	1928–29	Boston Bruins
1918–19	(Cancelled due to	1929–30	Montreal Canadiens
	influenza epidemic)	1930–31	Montreal Canadiens
1919–20	Ottawa Senators	1931–32	Toronto Maple Leafs
1920–21	Ottawa Senators	1932–33	New York Rangers
1921–22	Toronto St. Pats	1933–34	Chicago Black Hawks
1922–23	Ottawa Senators	1934–35	Montreal Maroons
1923–24	Montreal Canadiens	1935–36	Detroit Red Wings
1924–25	Victoria Cougars	1936–37	Detroit Red Wings
1925–26	Montreal Maroons	1937–38	Chicago Black Hawks
1926–27	Ottawa Senators	1938–39	Boston Bruins
1927–28	New York Rangers	1939–40	New York Rangers

STANLEY CUP WINNERS

1940–41	Boston Bruins	1956–57	Montreal Canadiens
1941–42	Toronto Maple Leafs	1957–58	Montreal Canadiens
1942–43	Detroit Red Wings	1958–59	Montreal Canadiens
1943–44	Montreal Canadiens	1959–60	Montreal Canadiens
1944–45	Toronto Maple Leafs	1960–61	Chicago Black Hawks
1945–46	Montreal Canadiens	1961–62	Toronto Maple Leafs
1946–47	Toronto Maple Leafs	1962–63	Toronto Maple Leafs
1947–48	Toronto Maple Leafs	1963–64	Toronto Maple Leafs
1948–49	Toronto Maple Leafs	1964–65	Montreal Canadiens
1949–50	Detroit Red Wings	1965–66	Montreal Canadiens
1950–51	Toronto Maple Leafs	1966–67	Toronto Maple Leafs
1951–52	Detroit Red Wings	1967–68	Montreal Canadiens
1952–53	Montreal Canadiens	1968–69	Montreal Canadiens
1953–54	Detroit Red Wings	1969–70	Boston Bruins
1954–55	Detroit Red Wings	1970–71	Montreal Canadiens
1955–56	Montreal Canadiens		

Béliveau 9

INDEX

Page numbers in italics refer to photographs.

Abel, Sid, 65
Abel, Taffy, 27
Adams, Jack, 64
Alexandrov, Veniamin, 74
All-Star Team (NHL), 24, 57, 63, 69, 70, 105
Amateur Hockey Association, 7
American League (hockey), 94
Apps, Syl, 60, 61
Arbour, Al, 91
Arena Gardens (Toronto), 29
Armstrong, George, 94, 114

Bailey, Irwin "Ace", 25–26
Balfour, Murray, 91
Barilko, Bill, 60, 62, *62*
Bathgate, Andy, 96
Bauer, Bobby, 48, *48*, 51
Baun, Bob, 94, 97, 114
Beliveau, Jean, 67–70, *68*, 122, 126
Bentley, Max, 60
Berenson, Gordon "Red", 121
Blair, Andy, 45
Blake, Hector "Toe," 55, 124–127, *125*
Boesch, Garth, 60
Boston Bruins, vii, 23, 24–26, 44–45, 47–52, *50*, 55–56, 61, 86, 103, 108–111, 116, 128–132
Boston Garden, 25
Boucher, Billy, 36, 37
Boucher, Frank, 27, 42

Bower, Johnny, 79, *81*, 83–84, 93, 94, 97, 113, 114, 115
Bowman, Scotty, 120–121
Brandon Wheat Kings, 13
Brewer, Carl, 94
Brimsek, Frank, 49
Broda, Walter "Turk", 59–60, 61, 62
Brooklyn (N.Y.) Skating Club hockey team, 85
Brown University, 85
Bruneteau, Moderre "Mud," 43, 44, 45–46
Buffalo Sabres, 133, 134
Bushnell, E. W., 3

Cahan, Larry, *117*
Cain, Herbie, 51
Calder, Frank, 44
Calder Trophy, 49, 82, 130
Campbell, Clarence, 76–78, *77*, 135
Canadian Amateur Hockey League, 12, 17
Canadian national amateur hockey team, 71–74, 86–87
Chabot, Lorne, 40, 42, 45–46
Chernyshev, Arkady, 74
Chicago Black Hawks, 10–11, 23, 36–37, 49, 60, 83, 89–92, 96, 101, 103, 106, 112, 113, 114, 116, 129, 130, 131, 135
Chicago Stadium, 10–11, 101

Christian, Billy, 86
Christian, Roger, 86
Clancy, Frank "King", 32, 113
Clapper, Dit, 49, 51
Cleary, Bill, 86, 87
Cleary, Bob, 86
Cleghorn, Odie, 18, 36
Cleghorn, Sprague, 18
Cleveland hockey team, 84
Cobalt (Ont.) hockey team, 18
Columbia University, 85
Conacher, Brian, 115
Conacher, Charlie, 32
Conacher, Roy, 49, 51
Connel, Alex, 40–41
Cook, Bill, 27
Cook, Bun, 27, 42
Cournoyer, Yvan, 70
Cowley, Bill, 49, 52
Crawford, Johnny, 49
Crescent Athletic Club hockey team, 85
Czechoslovakian national hockey team, 71, 73–74, 87, 135

Dawson City Klondikers, 13–14
Day, Clarence "Hap," 58–59, 61, 124
DeJordy, Denis, 114, 117
Delvecchio, Alex, 65
Detroit Cougars, 23
see also Detroit Red Wings
Detroit Olympics (hockey team), 46
Detroit Red Wings, 43, 45–46, 47, 52, 61, 62, 64–66, 76–77, 83, 89, 92, 96, 112, 116, 128, 131
Doraty, Ken, 43–45, 46
Duff, Dick, 94
Dumart, Woody, 48, 48, 51

Eastern Canadian Hockey Association, 17
Esposito, Phil, 129–130, 129, 131, 132
Esposito, Tony, 135
Ezinicki, Bill, 60

Federal Hockey League, 17
Ferguson, John, 70

Firsov, Anatoli, 74
Forrest, Albert, 13

Gagnon, Johnny, 37
Galt (Ont.) junior hockey team, 64–65
Gamble, Bruce, 113
Gardner, Cal, 61
Geoffrion, Bernie "Boom-Boom", 69, 76, 78, 100, 126
Getliffe, Ray, 49
Goldham, Bob, 65
Green, Ted, 131

Haileybury (Ont.) hockey team, 18
Hall, Glenn, vii, 79, 80, 83, 91–92, 114, 122, 123
Hamill, Red, 49
Hamilton (Ont.) hockey team, 23
Hammond, Col. John, 27, 28
Harris, Billy, 94
Hart Trophy, 33, 63, 70, 105
Harvard University, 85
Harvey, Doug, 69, 121, 126
Hay, Bill, 91
Hespeler (Ont.) junior hockey team, 90
Hill, Mel, 49, 51, 52
Hillman, Larry, 114
hockey
origin of, 3–6
seven-man teams, 8–9
world amateur competition, 71–74, 85–88, 135
Hockey Hall of Fame, 11
Hodge, Ken, 129, 130
Hollett, Flash, 49
Horner, Red, 25
Horton, Tim, 94, 114
Howe, Gordie, 63–66, 64, 70, 98–100, 99
Hull, Bobby, 90–92, 90, 98, 99, 101–102, 113, 114, 115, 129–30

ice skating,
origin of, 2–3
Imlach, George "Punch", 93–97, 112, 113, 115
Intercollegiate League, 85

Irvin, Dick, 32, 125
Ivan, Tommy, 89, 91

Jackson, Art, 51
Jackson, Harvey "Busher", 31–32
Johns Hopkins University, 85
Johnson, Ching, 27
Johnson, Paul, 86, 87
Johnson, Tom, 69, 126
Joliat, Auriel, 36, 37

Kelly, Red, 65, 94, 114
Kennedy, Ted, 60
Kenora Thistles, 14–16, 17
Keon, Dave, 94, 114
"Kid Line", 32
Kingston (Ont.), site of early hockey, 5, 6
Kingston Athletics, 6
Kingston Hockey Club, 6
Kitchener (Ont.) junior hockey team, 48
Kitchener-Waterloo Dutchmen, 87
Klukay, Joe, 60
Konovalenko, Victor, 74
"Kraut Line", 48, 48

Lach, Elmer, 55, 125
Lady Byng Trophy, 105, 125
Laperriere, Jacques, 70
Laycoe, Hal, 76
Lemaire, Jacques, 123
Leswick, Tony, 65
Lindsay, Bert, 18
Lindsay, Ted, 65
Litzenberger, Ed, 91
Livingstone, Eddie, 20
Los Angeles Kings, 116, 118
Lynn, Vic, 60

Magnuson, Keith, 135
Mahovlich, Frank, 94, 95
Maiorov, Eugeny, 72
Maki, Chico, 101
Maki, Wayne, 131
Malone, Joe, 20
Maniago, Cesare, 102
Maple Leaf Gardens (Toronto), 29–32, 30–31, 44, 95

Maritimes Professional League, 19
Marotte, Gil, 129
Martin, Pit, 129
Mayasich, Johnny, 86, 88
McArthur, Dalt, 127
McCartan, Jack, 86, 87, 88
McCormick, Hugh, 41
"McCullough" tube skates, 14
McDonald, Ab, 91
McGee, Frank, 12, 14, 15–16
McGill University (Montreal), 6
McKenney, Don, 96
Meeker, Howie, 60
Metz, Don, 60
Metz, Nick, 60
Mikita, Stan, 91, 103–107, 104, 113, 114, 130
"Million Dollar Line", 91
Minnesota North Stars, 84, 86, 116, 121
Minnesota, University of, 86
Montreal Amateur Athletic Association hockey team, 7, 8, 9
Montreal Canadiens, 10–11, 18, 20–21, 25, 33–38, 47, 54–57, 61–62, 67, 69–70, 75–78, 82, 84, 91–92, 96, 98, 100, 101, 113, 116, 121, 122–123, 124, 128, 130, 131
Montreal Forum, 38, 75
Montreal Maroons, 23, 40–42, 45–46
Montreal Victorias, 13
Montreal Wanderers, 9, 16, 18, 20
Moore, Dickie, 69, 121, 126
Morenz, Howie, 33–38, 34
Mortson, Gus, 60
Murdoch, Murray, 27
Murphy, Ron, 91

National Football League, 133
National Hockey Association (NHA), 9, 18–19, 20, 39
National Hockey League (NHL), 9
  American Division, 23, 40
Canadian Division, 23, 40
  East Division, 116
  expansion and growth, 116–119

origin of, 20
West Division, 116
Neilson, Jim, 102
Nesterenko, Eric, 91, 102
Nevin, Bob, 94
New Westminster (B.C.) hockey
    team, 19
New York Americans, 23
New York Athletic Club hockey
    team, 85
New York Rangers, 23, 27, 32, 37,
    39–42, 45, 49, 51–52, 53–54,
    55, 64, 84, 96, 101–102, 113,
    116, 121, 131
Norris, Jack, 129

Oakland Seals, 116
O'Brien, Ambrose, 18
Olmstead, Bert, 94
Olympic Games
    1956, 73
    1960, 73, 85, 86–88
Omaha (Neb.) hockey team, 65
Ontario Hockey Association Major
    Junior A Series, 133
Ontario Pro Hockey League, 17
Orr, Bobby, vii–ix, viii, 108–111,
    109, 128, 131, 132
Oshawa (Ont.) junior hockey team,
    110
Ottawa Capitals, 8, 9
    see also Ottawa Silver Seven
Ottawa Senators, 20–21
Ottawa Silver Seven, 9, 12–16
    see also Ottawa Capitals

Pacific Coast League, 19–20
Pappin, Jim, 115
Patrick, Frank, 18, 19, 39
Patrick, Lester, 18, 19, 39–42, 41
Patrick, Lynn, 120
Pavelich, Marty, 65
Penticton (B.C.) Vees, 73
Perrault, Gilbert, 134, 134
Pettinger, Red, 49
Petukhov, Stanislav, 88
Philadelphia Flyers, 116, 118, 121
Phillips, Tom, 14, 15–16, 17
Pilote, Pierre, 91

Pilous, Rudy, 91
Pittsburgh Penguins, 116
Pittsburgh Pirates (hockey team),
    23
Plante, Jacques, 69, 79, 80, 82–83,
    126
Portland, Jack, 49
Portland (Ore.) Rosebuds, 20
Powers, Eddie, 127
Primeau, Joe, 32
Princeton University, 85
"Production Line", 65
Pronovost, Marcel, 65, 112, 114
Pulford, Bob, 94, 115
"Punch Line", 55, 125

Quebec Aces, 69, 94
Quebec Bulldogs, 20, 21, 23
Quebec Citadels, 67
Quebec Coliseum, 68
Quebec hockey team (profes-
    sional), 118
Quebec Senior League, 94
Queen's University hockey team, 6

Ragulin, Alex, 74
Rat Portage hockey team, 13
    see also Kenora Thistles
Reardon, Terry, 51
Renfrew (Ont.) hockey team, 18,
    39
Richard, Henri, 122, 126
Richard, Maurice "Rocket", 54–
    57, 54, 56, 66, 69, 70, 75–76,
    78, 98–99, 125, 126
Riley, Jack, 86, 87
Ross, Art, 24, 44, 47, 49, 51
Ross Trophy, 105
Royal Military College hockey
    team, 6
Russian national hockey team, 71–
    74, 88, 135

St. Catharines (Ont.) junior hockey
    team, 90, 106
St. Laurent, Dollard, 91
St. Louis Blues, vii, 83, 116, 120–
    123, 124, 131–132
St. Nicholas Skating Club hockey
    team, 85

Salomon, Sidney, Jr., 120
Salomon, Sidney, III, 120
Sanderson, Derek, 130, 132
Sawchuk, Terry, 65, 79, *80*, 82, 112, 113, 114–115, *115*
Schmidt, Milt, 48, *48*, 51, 108–109, 128–129
Selke, Frank, 56, 126
Shock, Ron, 122
Shore, Eddie, 22, 24–26, 45, 48, 49, 51, 108
Sinden, Harry, 128
Skov, Glen, 65
Sloan, Tod, 62
Smith, Al, 113
Smith, Des, 51
Smith, Gary, 113
Smith, Normie, 45
Smythe, Conn, 27–32, *28*, 39, 44, 53, 58, 60, 61
Smythe Trophy, 123
Sologubov, Nicolai, 73, 87
Sports Illustrated magazine, 111
Springfield (Mass.) hockey team, 94, 118
Stanfield, Fred, 129, 130
Stanley, Allan, *54*, 94, 114
Stanley, Lord, of Preston, 7–8, *8*, 11
Stanley Cup
history of, 7–11
photographs of, *10*, *136*
Stratford (Ont.) amateur hockey team, 35
Stemkowski, Peter, 115
Stewart, Nels, 40, 42
Stewart, Ron, 94
Swedish national hockey team, 71, 73–74

Tallon, Dale, 134
Tarasov, Anatoli, 74
Taylor, Cyclone, 18
Thomas, Cy, 60
Thompson, Tiny, 45, 49

Thomson, Jim, 60
Toronto Arenas, 20–21
see also Toronto St. Patricks, Toronto Maple Leafs
Toronto Maple Leafs, 25–26, 27–32, 35, 43–45, 47, 51, 52, 53, 58–62, 84, 93–97, 101, 112–115, 116, 119, 130
Toronto Marlboroughs, 13
Toronto St. Patricks, 23, 28
name changed to Maple Leafs, 29
Toronto Shamrocks, 20
Tremblay, J. C., 70, 122

United States League, 65
United States Military Academy, 86
United States national hockey team, 73, 85–88

Vancouver Canucks, 133, 134
Vancouver Millionaires, *19*, 19, 21
Vasko, Elmer, 91
Vezina, Georges, 20
Vezina Trophy, 20, 49, 79, 82, 83
Victoria (B.C.) hockey team, 19

Watson, Harry, 60
West German national hockey team, 86
Western Canada League, 39
Westmount Arena (Montreal), 20
Wharram, Ken, 91
Williams, Tommy, 86, 88
Wilson, Bob, 89
Winnipeg Rowing Club hockey team, 13
World War II, effect on hockey, 53–54
Worsley, Lorne "Gump", 79, *81*, 84, 122

Yale University, 85

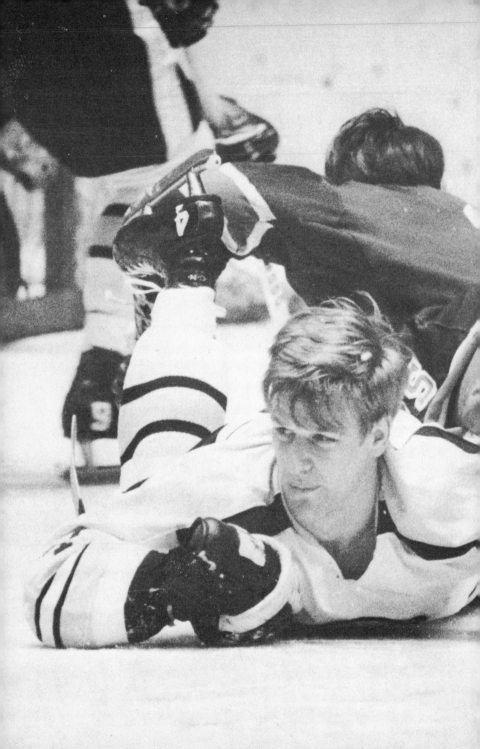